BY BILL GLEESON | PHOTOGRAPHS BY ALEX HAYDEN

weekends for two
IN THE PACIFIC NORTHWEST

THIRD EDITION • COMPLETELY REVISED AND UPDATED

50 ROMANTIC GETAWAYS

CHRONICLE BOOKS
SAN FRANCISCO

Text copyright © 2003 by Bill Gleeson.

Photographs copyright © 2003 by Alex Hayden.

Library of Congress Cataloging-in-Publication
Data available.

ISBN 0-8118-3532-4

Manufactured in China.

Designed and typeset by Deborah Bowman.

The author and photographer wish to thank
the following people for their assistance,
inspiration, and support:

Yvonne Gleeson

Susan Hayden

Doug Vann

Buddy Hayden

Elaine Kalber

Distributed in Canada by Raincoast Books
9050 Shaughnessy Street
Vancouver, British Columbia V6P 6E5

10 9 8 7 6 5 4 3 2 1

Chronicle Books LLC
85 Second Street
San Francisco, California 94105

www.chroniclebooks.com

Front cover: Rowena's Inn on the River,
British Columbia, page 112.

Table of Contents

Introduction

When my wife, Yvonne, and I first set out to compile *Weekends for Two in the Pacific Northwest,* we didn't anticipate the overwhelmingly positive response the book would receive from traveling romantics. Neither did we envision that more than a decade later we'd be retracing our steps for this third edition. In retrospect, however, it shouldn't have come as a big surprise—for a couple of good reasons.

First and foremost, while change is a constant in so many parts of our lives, romance never goes out of style. Second, when it comes to making romance, there's no setting like the Pacific Northwest. Whether the two of you enjoy sandy beaches, a craggy coastline, lush valleys, rolling foothills, remote islands, or rugged mountains, it's all here. Best of all, the romantic travel scene in this region keeps evolving and getting better. With this edition, we made way for fifteen new destinations, many of which were only the proverbial gleam in the innkeepers' eyes when we wrote the first edition.

Since the initial publication of *Weekends for Two in the Pacific Northwest,* our search for places of the heart has taken us across America. And as you might imagine, the inns and small hotels we've visited are as diverse as the nation itself. Along the way we've experienced the getaway gamut, from deliciously decadent to downright dirty and depressing. So, what makes for a romantic getaway? With the goal of ensuring a happily memorable experience, we've worked to refine the ingredients. Following are some of the features we like.

THE ELEMENTS OF ROMANCE

- Private bathrooms; a must in our opinion; we'll tell you if any are shared or detached.
- In-room fireplaces.
- Tubs and showers big enough for two; innkeepers in-the-know understand that a bathroom can be a romantic destination unto itself.
- Breakfast in bed; many traveling romantics don't fancy sharing a communal table with strangers.
- Feather beds and cushy comforters.
- Comfortable couches, chaises, or love seats; the bed shouldn't be the only piece of furniture where two can be together.
- Lamps, sconces, and candles; overhead lighting isn't particularly romantic.
- Private decks, patios, or balconies; most of us enjoy the inspiration of the outdoors.
- Rooms where smoking is never permitted.

Although few, if any, of our chosen destinations offer this complete list of romantic ingredients, each offers at least some of these features. And we endeavor to point them out, along with the occasional caveat concerning noise, size and location, furnishings, and so on.

THE PRICE OF ROMANCE

If a special occasion is worthy of a special bottle of wine or meal, it also deserves a memorable place to stay and play. Accordingly, you should be prepared to invest a little more for a romantic room fit for a special occasion.

To help you plan your getaway budget, approximate 2003 rate ranges are included for most of the rooms we describe. Keep in mind that these rates are always subject to change. Also, if you're booking a weekend trip, please note that many establishments require two-night minimum stays. Holidays often command three-night minimums.

Rates (per high-season, weekend night for two friendly people) are classified at the end of each listing using the following circa 2003 ranges, not including tax:

Moderate: Under $200
Expensive: $200 – $300
Deluxe: Over $300

FINAL NOTES

No payment was sought or accepted from any establishment in exchange for being included in this book. We make the decisions about which properties to include and how they're described.

Please understand that we cannot guarantee that these properties will maintain furnishings or standards as they existed at the time of our visit. We very much appreciate hearing from readers if their experience is at variance with our descriptions. Reader comments are carefully consulted and considered as we continually revise this book. Please send comments, suggestions, and ideas to Bill Gleeson in care of Chronicle Books at the address listed on the copyright page.

Smoking is not allowed in these properties unless otherwise noted. Food, wine, and flowers were sometimes added to rooms for our photographs. Some inns provide such amenities; others do not. Please ask when making a reservation whether these items are complimentary or whether they're provided for an extra charge.

DAYTIME DIVERSIONS

ASHLAND's famous Oregon Shakespeare Festival presents about twelve plays each year, from February through October. For ticket information, call (503) 482-4331. For a more romantic alternative, visit the intimate Oregon Cabaret Theatre at First and Hargadine Streets. Call (503) 488-2902.

About twelve miles away in historic JACKSONVILLE, the Britt Festivals draw thousands with an eclectic mix of performing and musical arts.

Downhill and cross-country ski areas are within a short drive of ASHLAND and BEND.

For information about Rogue and Klamath River trips, ask your innkeeper or call the Southern Oregon Visitors Association at (800) 448-4856.

The hulking Spruce Goose, built by the late aviator and reclusive industrialist Howard Hughes, is on permanent display at the Evergreen Aviation Museum in McMINNVILLE.

In PORTLAND, Heron Haus is near Washington Park, with its beautiful International Rose Test Gardens bursting with more than four hundred varieties of roses and covering four acres. The park also contains the Japanese Garden and a zoo. Nearby is the Nob Hill district (locals refer to it as Northwest Twenty-third), a trendy neighborhood of shops, restaurants, and vintage row houses.

The popular Saturday Market, held Saturday and Sunday mornings from March through Christmas takes place under the Burnside Bridge. Forest Park is the largest woodland city park in the United States.

TABLES FOR TWO

In the Ashland area, New Sammy's Cowboy Bistro (in nearby TALENT) belies its raucous-sounding name. It's actually an intimate establishment seating fewer than twenty and offering a menu of light French-country fare. Also recommended in ASHLAND are Monet and Chatêaulin, both French restaurants; and Primavera, which serves Mediterranean dishes. Wine-country visitors in-the-know cap off a day of wine touring with dinner at the Joel Palmer House in DAYTON, about eight miles from McMinnville. Nick's Italian Cafe in McMINNVILLE is another favorite.

McCormick & Schmick's Seafood Restaurant; Wildwood Restaurant and Bar; Genoa; and Toulouse are among PORTLAND's best dining choices.

WESTERN OREGON:
ASHLAND TO PORTLAND

ROMEO INN

295 Idaho Street
Ashland, OR 97520
Telephone: (541) 488-0884;
toll-free: (800) 915-8899
Web site: www.romeoinn.com

THE FACTS

Six rooms and suites, each with private bath, telephone, king-sized bed, and air-conditioning; three rooms with fireplaces. Complimentary full breakfast included; complimentary baked goods and soft drinks available in inn's refreshment center. Swimming pool and year-round heated spa. No disabled access. Two-night minimum stay required during weekends from June through September. Moderate to expensive.

GETTING THERE

From southbound Interstate 5, take exit 19 to Highway 99 and drive left through Ashland's downtown. Turn right on Gresham and left on Iowa. Turn right on Idaho and drive one block to inn. From northbound Interstate 5, take exit 11 and turn left on Sherman. Turn right on Iowa and left on Idaho to inn. Ashland is a five-and-a-half-hour drive from Portland.

ROMEO INN

Set on a pine-studded half acre in a quiet neighborhood, this handsome 1930s-era Cape Cod home was built on the side of a hill, affording lovely vistas of the Rogue Valley. A free-form swimming pool and spa are just outside the back door, adjacent to the garden, which constantly blooms with hundreds of varieties of flowers and herbs. The Oregon Shakespeare Festival grounds are only eight blocks away.

ROOMS FOR ROMANCE

The Stratford Suite (high $100 range), detached a few feet from the main house and reached by outside stairs, is the inn's most private and expensive accommodation. Decorated in lilac and peach tones, the suite has a vaulted ceiling, a separate living room with a cushy couch and chair, a woodburning marble fireplace, and a complete kitchen. The bathroom is equipped with a spa tub for two under a skylight. The suite offers views of the Rogue Valley, the Cascades, and the inn's garden.

In the main house, Cambridge Suite (upper $100 range) is the largest. This retreat has a private entrance through the back patio. The ceiling is vaulted, and the sitting area is furnished with overstuffed chairs set before a tiled fireplace.

Traveling romantics should take note that the bathroom for the second-floor Bristol Room is detached.

While many first-floor bed-and-breakfast guest rooms have all the privacy of a greenhouse, Romeo Inn's ground-floor accommodations—Canterbury and Windsor—feature private entrances off the side of the house. Canterbury (mid to upper $100 range) is decorated in dramatic burgundy tones and has a floor-to-ceiling woodburning brick fireplace.

Windsor (mid $100 range) has a partially canopied king-sized bed and two reading chairs. Both rooms have daybeds in addition to king-sized beds. Guests in these two rooms have garden views.

THE FACTS

*Five suites, each with private bath, spa tub for two, and gas
fireplace. Complimentary full breakfast included. Wine
and beer available on site. Communal spa and sauna. No
disabled access. Two-night minimum stay required during
weekends and holiday periods. Moderate to expensive.*

GETTING THERE

*From Interstate 5, 10 miles south of Ashland, take Mount
Ashland exit (exit 6) and drive west on Mount Ashland
Road for 6 miles to inn on right. Inn is approximately
15 miles north of California border.*

MOUNT ASHLAND INN
550 Mount Ashland Road
Ashland, OR 97520
Telephone: (541) 482-8707;
toll-free: (800) 830-7707
Web site: www.mtashlandinn.com

MOUNT ASHLAND INN

There are many Ashland inns, but only one Mount Ashland Inn. Unlike the town's older homes-turned-inns, Mount Ashland Inn is, well, a bit of a variation. Located about a half-hour south of town on the side of 7,500-foot Mount Ashland, this is a custom-crafted romantic mountain showplace that will take your breath away.

Built of gleaming locally harvested cedar logs, this chalet-style inn owes much of its charm to innkeepers Chuck and Laurel Biegert. Chuck handcrafted many of the impressive wood furnishings, while Laurel hand-crafts multicourse breakfasts for guests.

Cross-country skiing and hiking trails are accessible just outside the door of the inn. The Pacific Crest Trail runs along the property, and downhill skiing is three miles away. Available at no charge to guests are mountain bikes, cross-country skis, and snowshoes for local touring. A spacious outdoor spa with a view, as well as a dry-sauna house, await your return.

ROOMS FOR ROMANCE

Each of the inn's five rooms has a spa tub for two and a gas fireplace. Romantic hideaways don't get much better than the Sky Lakes Wilderness Suite (around $200), which consists of the top floor and features a wall of windows that face snow-capped Mount Shasta over the treetops. There are a rock fireplace, a king-sized bed, and a bathing area with a spa tub for two filled by a waterfall, as well as a two-headed shower.

Cottonwood Peak (mid $100 range) is a cozy ground-floor room with a queen-sized sleigh bed, antique furniture, a table and chairs, and a lovely forest view. A handmade quilt covers the bed.

Mount Shasta and Mount McLoughlin are framed by the windows of the Mount McLoughlin Suite (upper $100 range). The sitting area has a daybed and an antique bureau, and the sleeping area has a gas fireplace and a king-sized bed with a handmade quilt.

Sharing the third floor with the Mount McLoughlin Suite is the Mount Shasta Suite (mid $100 range), which offers views of its namesake peak from the queen-sized pencil-post bed and the sofa.

Stone and logs converge in the Mount Ashland Suite (mid $100 range), whose centerpiece is a hand-made queen-sized log bed.

THE FACTS

Nineteen rooms and suites, all with private bath; seven with soaking tubs for two; several with fireplaces. Fixed-price dinners served. Fishing shop on-site. Limited disabled access. The inn is closed January and February. Moderate to expensive.

GETTING THERE

From Interstate 5 at Roseburg, drive east on Highway 138 for 38 miles to inn on right. Inn is 70 miles from Crater Lake in summer, 120 miles in winter due to road closures. Plan on a four-hour drive from Portland.

STEAMBOAT INN
42705 N. Umpqua Highway
Steamboat, OR 97447-9703
Telephone: (800) 840-8825
Web site: www.thesteamboatinn.com

STEAMBOAT INN

True, Oregon's North Umpqua River is synonymous with steelhead. But at Steamboat Inn, which nestles along the river's banks, you're likely to find a good number of couples who are fishing for romance.

Built during the 1950s to serve the fishermen attracted by plentiful summer steelhead, the inn has grown over the years and today serves a varied clientele, from dedicated anglers to couples seeking a quiet and romantic weekend getaway.

Steamboat Inn is famous for its late-evening dinner, served a half-hour after dark daily during the summer and on weekends during winter months. Plan on spending approximately $40 per person for the meal.

ROOMS FOR ROMANCE

For the latter group, we recommend the two River suites (mid $200 range). Falls Suite is named for—and overlooks—the falls. Maple Ridge Suite overlooks the river's Maple Ridge pool.

These suites are equipped with king-sized beds and private decks; kitchenettes with utensils, two-burner stoves, and refrigerators; soaking tubs for two; and sitting rooms with fireplaces.

The inn's other romantically appropriate accommodations include eight cozy Streamside cabins (mid $100 range) situated below the main building. The pine-paneled cabins, each with queen-sized bed, share a covered river- and forest-view deck. These do not have cooking facilities.

Five Hideaway cottages (upper $100 range) are located about a half-mile upstream. These are equipped with a kitchenette, a separate bedroom with king-sized bed, a soaking tub for two, and a fireplace. They also include a sleeping loft and can accommodate up to four.

Three-bedroom ranch-style Water Houses (upper $100 range) occupy the site of what was once the North Umpqua Lodge. These units, which are within walking distance of great steelhead fishing, are perfect for families or three couples traveling together.

Steamboat Inn reports that the average North Umpqua steelhead weighs eight pounds. Although you may fish for steelhead in the North Umpqua year-round, the period from June through November is the most productive. The inn has a well-stocked fly-fishing equipment shop.

THE FACTS

One hundred units, each with private bath, kitchen, and gas fireplace. Fitness center and restaurant. No disabled access. Two-night minimum stay required during weekends; three-night minimum during holiday weekends. Moderate to deluxe.

GETTING THERE

From old Highway 97/Third Street in Bend, turn west on Mt. Washington Drive. Follow through two traffic circles to intersection of Mt. Washington Drive and Century Drive. Resort entrance is straight ahead. Directions vary depending on your approach to Bend. Check resort Web site for specifics.

MOUNT BACHELOR VILLAGE RESORT
19717 Mount Bachelor Drive
Bend, OR 97702
Telephone: (800) 452-9846
Web site: mtbachelorvillage.com

MOUNT BACHELOR VILLAGE RESORT

Mount Bachelor Village Resort is a perfect destination for couples who like to escape to the mountains without losing touch with civilization. Not only will you have access to the unspoiled rugged beauty of the Deschutes River, but you'll be close to Bend's myriad restaurants, shops, and movie theaters.

When they're not occupied by their owners, these privately owned vacation condominiums are available to folks like us who can only afford to visit for a weekend or, if we're fortunate, a week or two.

These units feature luxury furnishings and all the conveniences of home, and all have access (for a fee) to the Athletic Club of Bend, which is on the resort grounds. The club is equipped with indoor tennis, a rock-climbing wall, spa facilities, and an indoor pool. The Mount Bachelor ski area is twenty minutes away.

ROOMS FOR ROMANCE

Visitors can choose from what is called a "ski house" (these are actually condominiums) or a luxury condo within the River Ridge complex. The one- and two-bedroom ski houses, which dot the resort's core area, are near the year-round outdoor pool and spa. Rates range from around $100 for a one-bedroom unit to the high $100 range for a two-bedroom, two-bath condo.

Your romantic fires will definitely be kindled in a River Ridge condominium overlooking the river gorge and the distant mountains. A typical two-bedroom unit at River Ridge (mid $200 to low $300 range) has a sunken living/dining room combination, a kitchen, two bathrooms, and a large private view deck with a hot tub. One-bedroom condos are available for around $200.

THE FACTS

Seven rooms, each with private bath. Complimentary multicourse breakfast served at tables for two or more. Complimentary refreshments served in the afternoon. No disabled access. Two-night minimum stay required during weekends and holiday periods. Moderate to expensive.

GETTING THERE

From Portland (about 45 miles), drive south on Interstate 5 to Highway 99 West. Follow through Dundee and take Route 18, McMinnville bypass. Drive approximately 8 miles and take Highway 99 West/Corvallis/McMinnville exit. Turn right off exit road and drive a quarter mile, crossing Route 18 and heading straight onto Old Sheridan Road. Drive 1 mile and turn right on Peavine Road. Follow for 2 miles and turn left on Youngberg Hill Road. Follow for 1 mile to inn sign on right. Follow road up hill to inn.

YOUNGBERG HILL INN
10660 S.W. Youngberg Hill Road
McMinnville, OR 97128
Telephone: (503) 472-2727;
toll-free: (888) 657-8668
Web site: www.youngberghill.com

YOUNGBERG HILL INN

There are few Northwest regions that are more romantic than Oregon's wine country. And for winery-bound visitors seeking a romantic sleepover destination, Youngberg Hill Inn is the perfect match. With rooms offered at the time of our visit from the low to mid $100 range, Youngberg Hill is a romantic-getaway bargain.

Built just a decade or so ago as a bed-and-breakfast inn, but in the style of a gracious manor house, Youngberg Hill combines the comforts that today's travelers expect with a cozy, home-style atmosphere, complete with wraparound porches. Adding to the charm are a dozen acres of Pinot Noir vines set against a wonderful view of the Willamette Valley and the Coast Range. Kevin and Tasha Byrd, owners since 1997, have substantially redecorated and upgraded the property. They also craft a few hundred cases of estate Pinot Noir each year, and host popular "wine-maker dinners" in the winter and spring.

ROOMS FOR ROMANCE

For travelers on a budget, we recommend the Gamay Room (low to mid $100 range), which occupies a ground-floor corner and features a second door that opens onto the inn's deck. Inside are a handsome carved Victorian queen-sized bed, two chairs, and a gas fireplace. The bathroom has a large shower with a seat for two.

For those desiring a bit more space, the Jura Suite (upper $100 range) has a sitting room where two comfortable chairs are placed strategically before a row of windows that look out over the magnificent valley and beyond to Mount Hood and Mount Jefferson. The bedroom has a queen-sized bed, and the bathroom is equipped with a shower.

If only the best will do, ask for the Martini Suite (low to mid $200). Its list of romantic attributes include a king-sized bed, a woodburning fireplace, French doors opening to a private balcony with a knockout view, a separate sitting room, and a sumptuous bathroom featuring a shower and a huge spa tub for two.

THE FACTS

Six rooms, each with private bath, telephone, and television. Complimentary continental breakfast included. No disabled access. Moderate to deluxe.

GETTING THERE

Inn is located in hills of northwest Portland near intersection of Johnson and Westover Roads. Directions to Heron House are somewhat complex; they will be sent with a map after you make a reservation.

HERON HAUS
2545 Northwest Westover Road
Portland, OR 97210
Telephone: (503) 274-1846
Web site: www.heronhaus.com

For Portland visitors who prefer to spend their nights away from the madding crowd, we recommend Heron Haus, a stately three-story Tudor hybrid tucked away in a quiet, exclusive, older neighborhood above trendy Nob Hill. The home was converted into an inn by Julie Keppeler, a mother of four who returned to her native Northwest in the late 1980s after living for a time in Hawaii and Colorado.

Since our last Portland visit, cable car service has been added to Nob Hill. It runs from downtown through the Pearl District up to Twenty-Third and back.

ROOMS FOR ROMANCE

The guest rooms are furnished with a playful mix of traditional and contemporary pieces, along with a few family antiques. On the second floor is Kulia (which means *to desire* in Hawaiian), with shuttered windows offering a city view. The room (upper $100 range) has a queen-sized bed and a love seat as well as a raised spa with a view of the city.

Ko (Hawaiian for *sugar*), also on the second floor, is equipped with a king-sized bed and two sitting areas. The sexy shower in Ko's private bath is an original and boasts seven nozzles. The tariff for this room is in the low $100 range. If rented with the Kulia room's spa (when available), the room commands a rate in the mid $300 range.

The other second-floor room is Kanui (Hawaiian for *John*), a corner room (mid $100 range) with queen-sized bed and a view of Mounts Hood and St. Helens.

Away from it all on the third floor is the Manu (Hawaiian for *bird*) Suite, with a king-sized bed, a fireplace, a bay window, skylights, and two sitting areas; it's offered in the high $100 range. Guests here also have access to another room, with a four-poster double bed. Makua (Hawaiian for *elder*), also on the third floor, has a queen-sized bed, a bay window, skylights, and a fireplace. This room is priced in the mid $100 range.

Mahina (Hawaiian for *moonlight*) consists of the east end of the house on the third floor and overlooks the city toward Mounts Hood and St. Helens. Priced in the high $100 range, it holds a king-sized bed, a large sitting area, and a fireplace. In the bathroom is a rain-style shower, which provides a romantically drenching spray.

DAYTIME DIVERSIONS

The Oregon Coast Association publishes a coastal travel
guide that includes maps and details about whale watching, agate hunting, and lighthouse touring, among other
activities. For a free copy, write to the Oregon Coast
Association, P.O. Box 670, Oregon Coast, OR 97365.

NORTH OF NEWPORT is Yaquina Head Lighthouse,
which commands a romantic setting on a coastal bluff.
This is also a great spot for a beach walk.

The Cape Perpetua Scenic Area near YACHATS offers
coastal and forest hiking trails that range in length from a few
hundred yards to ten miles. On a clear day, a visit to Saint
Perpetua Viewpoint will reward you with 150-mile views.

While it's not one of the state's most romantic spots,
the Oregon Coast Aquarium in NEWPORT is definitely
worth a visit.

TABLES FOR TWO

On the northern coast, our innkeepers recommend Café
de la Mer in CANNON BEACH, and Jarboe's near the Inn
at Manzanita. In DEPOE BAY, we enjoyed the seafood
dishes and ocean vistas at Tidal Raves on Highway 101.
Closer to LINCOLN CITY, but still accessible from Depoe
Bay, is Bay House, also for seafood on Highway 101.

The Windward Inn Restaurant, two miles north of
FLORENCE on Highway 101, is known for its seafood and
shellfish, as well as a wide selection of Pacific Northwest wines.

THE OREGON COAST

THE FACTS

Amenities include fresh flowers in season and a complimentary bottle of Oregon wine upon arrival. No disabled access. Moonset Cottage: Two-night minimum; expensive. Rose Cottage: No multinight stay required; moderate.

GETTING THERE

Obtain keys at 216 Maple Street, Florence. From Highway 101, turn east onto Maple Street (north of the bridge) and follow to First and Maple Streets in Old Town Florence, one block north of bayfront. Moonset Cottage is 9 miles north of Florence on Highway 101. Florence is approximately 160 miles southwest of Portland.

MOONSET AND ROSE COTTAGES
c/o 216 Maple Street (P.O. Box 1892)
Florence, OR 97439
Telephone: (800) 768-9488
Web sites: www.touroregon.com/moonset/ or
www.moonsetromance.com

MOONSET AND ROSE COTTAGES

Set high at the edge of a one-acre ocean-view meadow, Moonset Cottage is a two-level, octagon-shaped, self-contained lovers' hideaway with nearly every accessory a romantic could hope for.

After making the scenic nine-mile drive north from Florence, guests enter the property through a wooden gate and follow a grass and gravel drive that ends at Moonset's carport. From here, a winding stairway leads to the cabin's living area, furnished with a love seat, a woodburning stove, and a compact disc/cassette stereo system. A multiwindowed view sweeps from the meadow and surrounding forest to the ocean. Adjacent Lily Lake is also visible.

A couple of steps down from the living area is the tiled kitchen, complete with an oven, a Jenn-Air range, pots and pans, dishes, cutlery, and even a coffee grinder and coffee beans. Guests also receive a complimentary bottle of Oregon wine and fresh flowers.

Just above the kitchen is a cozy sleeping loft reached by a short ladder. The king-sized bed is covered with a goose-down comforter. The ocean is visible through the living-area windows. The bathroom is equipped with a tiled shower. An ocean-view spa, shower, and sauna are located on the deck.

The daily rate for Moonset Cottage is around $200, with a two-night minimum stay required.

If Moonset Cottage is too expensive or is unavailable (it's often booked months in advance), you might want to consider tiny Rose Cottage, which sits behind Johnson House Bed and Breakfast in Florence. Moonset and Rose Cottages are owned by the same family.

Guests follow a stone path behind the main building to reach Rose Cottage (low $100 range), which is set among rosebushes. Inside is a queen-sized bed, two chairs, and a deep, long clawfoot tub. This 1920s-era cottage is decorated with rose-print wallpaper and framed antique rose prints. There's a porch with chairs out front. Breakfast is served to guests in this unit.

THE FACTS

Six rooms, each with private bath and outdoor sitting area; four with tubs for two. Complimentary full breakfast served at tables for two. No disabled access. Two-night minimum stay required during weekends; three-night minimum during holiday periods. Moderate to expensive.

GETTING THERE

Inn is on ocean side of Highway 101, between mile markers 171 and 172, 7 miles south of Yachats and 18 miles north of Florence.

SEA QUEST BED AND BREAKFAST

95354 Highway 101 (P.O. Box 448)
Yachats, OR 97498
Telephone: (541) 547-3782
Web site: www.seaq.com

SEA QUEST BED AND BREAKFAST

We mistakenly believed we had thoroughly covered the Oregon coast's romantic getaway possibilities until a couple of thoughtful readers shared this oceanfront discovery with us.

Formerly a private residence, the contemporary two-story structure, which overlooks the ocean and the outlet of Ten Mile Creek, was completely remodeled by innkeepers Elaine Ireland and George Rozsa. In addition to adding lots of windows to take advantage of the dazzling ocean views, the owners refitted the contemporary two-story structure to accommodate six guest rooms, each offering a private entrance. Four rooms have spa tubs for two.

The inn's great room, with its dramatic brick and stone fireplace, is on the second level, along with a big kitchen, site of the Sea Quest's impressive buffet breakfast. There's also a retreat for guests on the ground floor. Baked goods and coffee are always available.

ROOMS FOR ROMANCE

Since our first visit, a fabulous new suite (called The Sweete) has been created. Priced in the low $300 range per night, this romantic one-thousand-square-foot room features a king-sized canopy bed, overstuffed chairs, a woodburning fireplace, a corner spa tub for two, and an expansive, floor-to-ceiling ocean view.

Situated about one hundred feet from the ocean, room 1 (upper $100 range) has a queen-sized antique bed, two sitting chairs, an outdoor seating area, and a bathroom where a spa tub for two looks out through a shuttered window across the room to the ocean. There's also a separate shower.

Room 2 (upper $100 range) has a queen-sized bent-willow bed and an outdoor sitting area. This room also has a shower, as well as a spa tub for two with an ocean view.

Room 3 (upper $100 range) has a queen-sized sleigh bed, a spa tub for two, two wicker chairs, and an ocean-view porch.

Room 4 occupies a first-floor corner and is furnished with a high, queen-sized antique bed and a sitting area with an easy chair. The large bathroom has a spa tub for two and a separate shower. This room boasts a view of the mountains and the ocean, and has a small ocean-view garden area furnished with chairs.

Room 5 (mid $100 range) has a queen-sized antique bed, a bathroom with a shower, an easy chair, and a private sitting area and garden.

THE FACTS

Fourteen rooms, each with private bath; twelve with fire-places and outdoor spa tubs for two. Complimentary continental breakfast. No disabled access. No minimum night stay requirement. Moderate to deluxe.

GETTING THERE

From Portland, drive west on Highway 99. At McMinnville, drive southwest on Highway 18. At Lincoln City, drive south on Highway 101. In Depoe Bay, drive west on Ellingson. Channel House is located one block west of Highway 101 at south end of Depoe Bay Bridge.

CHANNEL HOUSE BED-AND-BREAKFAST INN
35 Ellingson Street (P.O. Box 56)
Depoe Bay, OR 97341
Telephone: (541) 765-2140;
toll-free: (800) 447-2140
Web site: www.channelhouse.com

CHANNEL HOUSE BED-AND-BREAKFAST INN

Don't be dissuaded by this inn's nondescript exterior or its location along Depoe Bay's commercial strip. Step inside most any guest room and prepare to be overwhelmed—in a most romantic way. Gazing from your bed through a wall of glass, the ocean is all you'll see.

Our favorite Oregon coast destination, Channel House is housed in a newer building, shingled and square. The furnishings are contemporary, and the bathrooms are spacious. Most every room has a private deck, a fireplace, and a spa tub.

ROOMS FOR ROMANCE

The inn sits on the ocean's edge directly adjacent to the Jaws, the ominous nickname given to the rugged, narrow channel that connects the sea with Depoe Bay harbor. Consequently, the ocean-facing rooms on the inn's north side come with a bonus view.

If you enjoy having room to spread out, we suggest Cuckoo's Nest (upper $200 range) on the inn's top floor. The suite has its own full kitchen with a refrigerator, and there are gas fireplaces in the living room and bedroom, along with a couch. The bathroom holds a double-headed shower for two. A private spa is outside on the deck.

Channel Watch is a large suite with a full kitchen and a fireplace in the bedroom and living room. Depending on the time of your visit, you might catch a glimpse of a passing whale from your private whirlpool spa on the deck. This room is offered in the upper $200 range.

The Captain's Quarters and The Bridge (mid $200 range) both offer particularly private decks and spas. There are also three other oceanfront rooms with small deck spas priced at around $200.

Salt Air (mid $200 range), on the ground floor, is the only suite with a king-sized bed. Equipped with a spa and a gas fireplace, it has separate living and sleeping rooms connected by French doors. A tub for two is situated on the large deck.

Whale Watch (mid $200 range) is located on the channel and also fronts the ocean. The room has a wet bar, a gas fireplace, a queen-sized bed, a couch, and a whirlpool spa on the deck. The Admiral's Suite is similarly styled, but is one level higher. The side-facing Crow's Nest and Aft Suite have the least impressive ocean views.

Although the television in each room is connected to a premium movie channel, our hunch is that you'll be tuned to the live drama unfolding outside your window.

THE FACTS

Thirty rooms, each with private bath with spa tub, gas fire-place, videocassette player, deck, and ocean view; some with full kitchens. Complimentary continental breakfast and morning paper delivered to your room; complimentary wine and refreshments served in afternoon. Restaurant. Library. Disabled access. Two-night minimum stay required during summer weekends and certain holiday periods. Moderate to deluxe.

GETTING THERE

From Highway 101 in Lincoln City, turn east into hotel parking area on Inlet Court, just north of D River Beach Wayside.

O'DYSIUS HOTEL

120 N.W. Inlet Court
Lincoln City, OR 97367
Telephone: (541) 994-4121;
toll-free: (800) 869-8069
Web site: www.odysius.com

O'DYSIUS HOTEL

Oregon coast travelers who have lamented the lack of a suitably romantic destination in Lincoln City have reason to return, thanks to the opening of the luxurious O'dysius Hotel. It's a charming oasis in this land of outlet shops and anonymous lodgings.

Situated just above the D River Wayside with direct access to eight miles of flat, sandy beach, the O'dysius is a multistoried hotel with a facade of stucco and stone. Its styling is intended to reflect that of a small European boutique hotel.

ROOMS FOR ROMANCE

Although there are multiple room categories at the O'dysius, each has a slate entry, comfortable over-stuffed furnishings, tasteful art, an ocean view, a gas fireplace, a videocassette player, and a spa tub. You'll also be treated to robes, slippers, down duvets, and feather pillows. Standard rooms with these amenities are priced in the mid $100 range.

Grand Deluxe rooms (around $200) have the most private balconies, while Parlor Suites (low $200 range) offer secluded balconies as well as separate bedrooms and kitchenettes.

The Grand Suite (low $300 range) has all the above features as well as two bedrooms and a large spa tub for two in the master bedroom.

INN AT MANZANITA

67 Laneda (P.O. Box 243)
Manzanita, OR 97130
Telephone: (503) 368-6754
Web site: www.neahkahnie.net

THE FACTS

Thirteen rooms, each with private bath, gas fireplace, spa tub for two, television, videocassette player, and refrigerator. Two-night minimum required on weekends and from Memorial Day through Labor Day; three-night minimum required during some holiday periods. Limited disabled access. Moderate.

GETTING THERE

From Portland, take Highway 26 west to Highway 101. Drive south on Highway 101 for 12 miles to Manzanita. Turn west at Manzanita sign and follow one-half mile to inn on right. Manzanita is 80 miles from Portland.

INN AT MANZANITA

Set behind a stand of spindly pine and spruce along a seven-mile stretch of beach, the shingled Inn at Manzanita was obviously created with romance in mind. Every couple is treated like newlyweds. Unlike many hostelries that outfit only one or two honeymoon suites with the most sensuous accessories, the Inn at Manzanita has bestowed these features on every room in the house. And they don't command those high honeymoon suite rates, either. At the time of our visit, rates started in the low $100 range, topping out in the mid $100 range.

ROOMS FOR ROMANCE

Each of the thirteen rooms is equipped with a gas fireplace, a spa tub for two, an ocean-view deck, and a small refrigerator to chill that special bottle of champagne you brought along.

Spread among two fourplex units (two rooms on top, two on the bottom), eight rooms boast corner windows and ocean-view decks. Inside some rooms, furnishings are minimal, with a pair of chairs providing the only seating aside from the bed. All beds are queen-sized.

The guest rooms in a newer building have larger floor plans and are equipped with a couch and a captain's bed placed in a sunlit alcove. The top-floor rooms in this unit (Starseeker and West-erner) also have skylights.

The original building, constructed in the mid-1980s, is more standard, but the rooms have high ceilings; the second-floor rooms here (Woodsman and Explorer) have wonderful views.

The lowest rates are charged for ground-floor rooms. It costs a few dollars more to stay in the second-floor units.

The rooms in the newer three-unit building have ocean views and decks. We have heard from a few readers who found these rooms to be a bit too close to Laneda Avenue.

TURK'S LODGINGS

Highway 101 (P.O. Box 482)
Cannon Beach, OR 97110
Telephone: (503) 436-1809
Web site:
www.clatsop.com/turkslodging/house.html

THE FACTS

*No disabled access. Two- or three-night minimum stay
required during certain times of year. Moderate to deluxe.*

GETTING THERE

*From Highway 101, approximately 2 miles south of Cannon
Beach and one hundred feet south of milepost marker 32,
turn east into property driveway at sign reading "50 Turk's."*

Even if you've cozied up in a room in a luxurious inn on the coast, there's something about a private ocean-view house or cottage that just can't be bested. Don't worry if you can't afford to buy your own. Turk's Lodgings can set the two of you up for a weekend—or a week.

ROOMS FOR ROMANCE

Bob and Carole Turk built the dramatic, partially stilted House in the Trees as their home. (They were married on the deck overlooking the ocean.) These days, the home is our favorite of a trio of accommodations operated by the Turks for discerning travelers. It's also a favorite of our readers, and weekends are often booked well in advance. During the summer, the nightly rate is in the mid $300 range; the winter rate is in the low $200 range.

Inside are soaring ceilings, expansive windows, and a stone fireplace. An ocean-view deck wraps around two sides of the house. The step-down full kitchen is equipped with a wood stove and a gas restaurant stove. Just off the deck is a wicker-furnished sunroom. There's also a home theater system and a DVD player.

The master bedroom is a romantic dream come true. It's a split-level affair with a king-sized bed, a desk, and a spa tub for two on the lower level. The bed and spa are set against windows that look out through trees to the ocean. You'll also be able to view the sea from both the living room and master bedroom, and there's a rock-walled, blue-tiled shower for two, with a view of the ocean.

The other bedroom is a loft overlooking the kitchen. The loft bedroom is furnished with wicker furniture and a king- as well as a queen-sized bed. Large windows overlook the sea.

If you plan to share the house with another couple, be aware that the master bedroom is much better equipped for romance and is more private than the loft bedroom. To make sure everyone leaves happy and satisfied, you might want to consider trading bedrooms if you're staying for more than one night.

In addition to the House in the Trees, the Turks make available the Cottage in the Trees and Studio in the Trees. The one-bedroom Cottage (low $200 range in summer; mid $100 range in winter) has a full kitchen, a wood stove, a cable television, a DVD player, decks, ocean and mountain views, and a one-person spa tub.

The Studio (low to mid $100 range in summer; around $100 in winter) is a cozy studio-sized accommodation with a queen-sized bed, a couch, a DVD player, and a kitchenette. It also offers a view of the ocean.

DAYTIME DIVERSIONS

If you're staying at the Salish Lodge and it's a dry day, leave the crowds at the top of SNOQUALMIE FALLS and take the half-hour walk down the trail to the base of the waterfall for a truly romantic view. Golfers can choose from four area courses, and bicyclists have access to the Ski Acres Mountain Bike Center. Downhill and cross-country ski areas are located less than a half-hour from the lodge. There's a name-brand discount shopping center in nearby NORTH BEND.

In the LEAVENWORTH AREA, cross-country skiers can take advantage of groomed town trails or Lake Wenatchee State Park. For downhill skiing, try nearby Stevens Pass or the less-crowded Mission Ridge. During warmer weekends, there are art shows in the village park. The lush nine-acre Ohme Gardens, near WENATCHEE, sits high on a rocky bluff and represents more than sixty years of work by the Ohme family. Romantics will enjoy a Wenatchee Riverfront Park stroll. There are also a couple of golf courses in the LEAVENWORTH AREA, one of which is within walking distance of All Seasons River Inn Bed and Breakfast.

Sun Mountain Lodge guests have little reason to leave the resort grounds, considering the wealth of year-round recreational activities available there. For a change of scenery, take the quick drive to historic WINTHROP, a restored Gold Rush-era town with wooden sidewalks, Washington's oldest saloon, and a history museum. There's a golf course in Winthrop.

TABLES FOR TWO

SNOQUALMIE is small, so the restaurant at the Salish Lodge is probably the best bet. It's very romantic, though a bit pricey. The Herb Farm in nearby FALL CITY has a nice restaurant that serves a rather expensive multicourse lunch. The Brown Bag Restaurant and Bakery in nearby CARNATION serves lunch and dinner on certain days.

In LEAVENWORTH, Lorraine's Edel Haus serves a five-course dinner exclusively for guests of All Seasons River Inn Bed and Breakfast. Guests are chauffeured and wined and dined for a three-hour feast. Sun Mountain Lodge also has a restaurant.

Birchfield Manor Country Inn and Gasperetti's Restaurant are recommended in YAKIMA.

THE CASCADES
AND SOUTHERN WASHINGTON

BIRCHFIELD MANOR COUNTRY INN

2018 Birchfield Road
Yakima, WA 98901
Telephone: (509) 452-1960;
toll-free: (800) 375-3420
Web site: www.birchfieldmanor.com

THE FACTS

Eleven rooms, each with private bath; four with gas fire-places; eight with spa tubs for two. Complimentary full breakfast served at a communal table or in your room. Swimming pool and restaurant. Disabled access. No mini-mum night stay requirement. Moderate to expensive.

GETTING THERE

From Interstate 82, take Highway 24 (exit 34) east and follow for 2 miles. Turn right on Birchfield Road and follow a quarter mile to first house on right.

For many traveling romantics, including the two of us, a fine dinner and sumptuous accommodations are the most important ingredients of a memorable romantic getaway. Unfortunately, it's rare that we discover noteworthy pairings of food and lodging under one roof. That's what makes Birchfield Manor such a traveler's treasure.

The dining experience alone is worth a drive. European-trained chef-owner Wil Masset prepares innovative and memorable dinners in the country setting of this fine historic home. The wine list, which features Yakima Valley vintages, is equally impressive. Dinners are served Thursday through Saturday. Guests staying in the cottage rooms may have dinner or hors d'oeuvre plates served in their guest rooms.

Although Birchfield Manor initially derived its reputation for its kitchen, it's also gaining quite a following for its romantic accommodations, which have expanded in recent years to include contemporary-style rooms with fireplaces and whirlpool tubs for two.

ROOMS FOR ROMANCE

There are five bedrooms in the original manor house, and four have spa tubs for two and showers. The largest is Elizabeth, which has a king-sized bed, a sitting area, a separate dressing room, and a view of the swimming pool. These rooms are priced in the mid $100 range.

For a romantic splurge, we highly recommend the six cottage rooms, five of which have king-sized beds. Hunters Glen and Rose Sunset (upper $100 range) have showers and tubs for two, while the Vineyard and Panorama Rooms (around $200) have tubs for two and showers with steam saunas.

In the original manor house, rooms 3 and 4 (mid $100 range) have spa tubs for two, double-head showers, fireplaces, televisions, and private decks boasting valley views. Room 2 (low $100 range) has a shower for two.

THE FACTS

Ninety-one rooms and suites, each with private bath. All rooms equipped with woodburning fireplace, spa tub for two, honor bar, television, telephone; and oversized towels. Complimentary tea and cookies served every afternoon. Guests have complimentary use of trail bikes. Restaurant, lounge, gift shop, fitness room, sports court, and spa. Disabled access. Smoking not permitted in rooms. Expensive to deluxe.

GETTING THERE

From Interstate 90, take exit 25 and follow signs to Snoqualmie Falls, about 3 miles from interstate. Lodge is approximately forty minutes by car from Seattle.

SALISH LODGE AND SPA
6501 Railroad Avenue (P.O. Box 1109)
Snoqualmie, WA 98065
Telephone: (425) 888-2556;
toll-free: (800) 826-6124
Web site: www.salishlodge.com

We watched tourists by the car and busload jockey for a spot at the railing, snap a photo of frothy Snoqualmie Falls, gape for a minute or two, then drive away. Unfortunately, they're missing the best part: a night at the Salish (pronounced SAY-lish) Lodge, which merits a strong A on our romantic scorecard.

The centerpiece of the short-lived and cult-favorite television show *Twin Peaks,* the Salish is perched right at the edge of the roaring falls, enjoying one of the most spectacular settings in the Northwest.

Don't worry that the heavy tourist traffic around the falls will threaten your privacy as a guest at the lodge. Even though the public areas bustle with curious daytrippers and restaurant diners, the doors to the guest floors are locked; only you and the other guests will have keys to what lies within.

Keep in mind that the lodge is perched along the river at the edge of Snoqualmie Falls, so don't expect to see the waterfall from your guest room. The best views of the cascade are offered from nearby public vista points. For an even more impressive view, take the winding walking trail down to the base of the 268-foot falls. The lodge's restaurant also offers stirring vistas.

If the setting and the inn's romantic and relaxing rooms don't sufficiently reinvigorate your bodies and souls, the Salish also operates a spa offering stone massages, facials, body wraps, and hand and foot treatments.

ROOMS FOR ROMANCE

Our advice for making the most of a romantic visit is to book a river-view room that will allow you to gaze at the water, lulled by the ever-present roar of the falls. The best rooms—120, 220, 324, and 423—are dramatic corner spots that overlook the edge of the misty falls and the green mountains and forests beyond. Luxury does carry a price, however, and these large suites, all with lots of windows and window seats, carry nightly tariffs ranging from $600 to $1000.

Other river-view rooms start in the mid $200 range. Rooms with a courtyard view are a few dollars less. Honeymoon packages are also available. Rates drop considerably midweek. As you move toward the other end of the building, the adjacent historic Puget Power station competes somewhat with the natural vistas.

Our river-view retreat, room 418, represented a typical sampling of the Salish's accommodations. The room is long, with the bathroom situated at one end. Next to the spa tub for two is a window that, when opened, looks across the river to a beautiful wall of trees.

Cozy chairs, original art, a cushioned long window seat, a ready-to-light fireplace, and a king-sized feather bed with a goose-down comforter and a view completed the setting.

Six rooms, each with private bath, riverfront deck, and spa tub for two. Complimentary full breakfast; hot cider served on arrival during winter; complimentary snack served each evening. Bicycles available to guests at no charge. No disabled access. Two-night minimum stay required on weekends and holidays. Moderate.

From Highway 2 in Leavenworth, turn south on Icicle Road and travel 1 mile to bridge. Inn is second house on left after bridge. Leavenworth is two and a quarter hours from Seattle.

ALL SEASONS RIVER INN BED AND BREAKFAST

8751 Icicle Road
Leavenworth, WA 98826
Telephone: (509) 548-1425;
toll-free: (800) 254-0555
Web site: www.allseasonsriverinn.com

ALL SEASONS RIVER INN BED AND BREAKFAST

A three-year search throughout the Northwest for the perfect setting for their bed-and-breakfast inn brought Jeff and Kathy Falconer to a lovely spot along the evergreen waters of the Wenatchee River. It was here that they set about creating All Seasons River Inn, incorporating many of the design ideas they had collected during ten years of romantic travels.

The three-story cedar-sided inn contains a large living room with a river-view bay window, a fireplace, a game room, and an upstairs television room. On warm summer days, guests often head down to the inn's private beach for a swim in the Wenatchee River.

ROOMS FOR ROMANCE

The inn's Enchantment Suite, offered in the mid $100 range, not only has a large spa tub in the room but a separate bathroom with a shower for two. The room boasts a bay-windowed seating area with an antique sofa and also contains a king-sized antique poster bed and a gas fireplace.

You'll be treated to sweeping views of the river from Serenity Suite (mid $100 range), a room that features a gas fireplace, a private deck, a carved oak bed, a wicker love seat, and a corner spa tub for two facing the bed.

In River Bend, guests can enjoy the view from two cushy mauve chairs or the ornately carved Queen Anne bed. This room, whose shower is big enough for two, is offered for around $100.

The inn's most romantic accommodation is the Evergreen Suite (high $100 range), which overlooks the river and pampers guests with creature comforts that include a gas fireplace, a river-view love seat, and a king-sized, carved oak bed. This suite, pictured at left, also features an arched entry framing a sitting room furnished with a bay window and a large spa tub.

THE FACTS

Six suites, each with private bath, spa tub, gas fireplace, private deck, compact disc and DVD players, and refrigerator with complimentary refreshments. Complimentary full breakfast served at communal table. Complimentary refreshments served in the afternoon. No disabled access. Two-night minimum stay required during weekends and from peak season, which runs from May through October, and also includes month of December. Three-night minimum stay required during holiday periods. Single-night stays available Sunday through Thursday during other nonpeak periods. Expensive.

GETTING THERE

From Highway 2 south of Leavenworth, drive west on East Leavenworth Road for 1 mile to inn sign. Turn right and follow lane.

RUN OF THE RIVER
9308 East Leavenworth Road
(P.O. Box 285)
Leavenworth, WA 98826
Telephone: (509) 548-7171;
toll-free: (800) 288-6491
Web site: www.runoftheriver.com

RUN OF THE RIVER

"Some places call a room with a bed and two chairs a suite," says Run of the River proprietor Monty Turner. "This isn't that," he adds, savoring the obvious understatement.

Truly a one-of-a-kind property, Run of the River expertly combines natural beauty (a river really does run through it), whimsy (old bicycles are integrated into the decor), rustic charm (log walls, and chairs made of branches), and loads of comfort and elegance (plush beds, spa tubs, and more).

ROOMS FOR ROMANCE

Run of the River celebrated the millennium with a dramatic face-lift of its already impressive guest rooms, combining six rooms to create three stunning suites, and adding two brand-new romantic hideaways.

Among the most luxurious is the spacious Kingfisher (mid $200 range), which Monty and his wife Karen describe as "luxury in log." This downstairs suite features a comfy sitting area, and a gas fireplace set against a backdrop of river rock. The spa tub for two also has a stone surround.

Also the result of combining two rooms is Enchantments (mid $200 range), which offers two decks offering inspiring views of the adjacent wildlife refuge, the river, and the mountains beyond. Guests reach this private second-floor hideaway via private outdoor stairs. The Up the Creek room (low $200 range) has a sitting area and spa for two with a view, and is also accessed via private stairs (inside).

Great Northwest (low $200 range) has a river view and a covered wraparound deck that beckons year-round. It also has a view spa tub for two framed with river rock. Osprey and Hit the Trail (low $200 range) are located above Great Northwest. Both of these view rooms feature "play lofts." Let the fun and games begin.

If having "the run of the river" isn't sufficient to keep the two of you occupied, the Leavenworth area bursts with activities year-round. In the winter there are skiing at Mission Ridge or Stevens Pass, snowshoeing, sleigh rides, and cross-country skiing. The inn offers winter fun packages. During the warmer months, you can borrow a mountain bike from the inn and make a romantic memory at Leavenworth Summer Theater.

THE FACTS

*One hundred fifteen rooms and cabins, each with private
bath; many with fireplaces and spa tubs for two. Restaurant,
tennis courts, exercise room, boat and mountain bike rentals,
stables, ice-skating rink, hiking and cross-country ski trails,
lake, four swimming pools, spas, and day spa services.
Disabled access. Two-night minimum stay on weekends;
three-night minimum stay required during holiday periods.
Moderate to deluxe.*

GETTING THERE

*From Wenatchee, drive north on Highway 97 along the
Columbia River to Highway 153 junction at Pateros. Drive
north on Highway 153 for 40 miles and turn left on Twin
Lakes Road. Follow signs for 8 miles to lodge. North Cascades
Highway is open April through November for a shorter trip
to Sun Mountain. From Interstate 5, drive east on Highway
20 at Burlington to Winthrop. From Winthrop, follow signs
for 9 miles to lodge.*

SUN MOUNTAIN LODGE
P.O. Box 1000
Winthrop, WA 98862
Telephone: (509) 996-2211;
toll-free: (800) 572-0493
Web site:
www.sunmountainlodge.com

SUN MOUNTAIN LODGE

Unlike most of the intimate, couples-oriented destinations featured in this book, Sun Mountain Lodge is a bustling year-round resort that markets itself as a family destination. However, traveling twosomes who like to combine romance with recreation will find Sun Mountain a perfect destination.

While Sun Mountain Lodge is designed for year-round enjoyment, a winter weekend here must rank as among the Northwest's most romantic getaways. A dip in one of the heated spas, ice skating hand-in-hand, an intimate sleigh ride through the snow—need we say more?

ROOMS FOR ROMANCE

Updated, remodeled, and expanded in recent years, the property offers a mix of lodging options. There are more than one hundred rooms and lakeside cabins to choose from. And the lodge takes pride in proclaiming that none has a television.

Our most highly recommended romantic retreats are found in the newer Mount Robinson building. These rooms (around $200) and one-bedroom suites (mid $200 range) have draped king-sized beds, gas fireplaces, private decks, wet bars, sitting areas, and spa tubs situated so as to take advantage of nice views of Mounts Robinson and Gardner.

In the Gardner wing, the guest rooms boast lava rock fireplaces, furnishings of hand-hewn birch and willow, exposed beams, hand-painted bedspreads, view decks, wet bars, and original artwork by local artisans. The rooms here command tariffs in the mid $100 range, while suites can range upwards of $200. Deluxe rooms in the lodge are priced in the mid $100 range.

The Patterson Lake cabins (mid $100 range) are situated next to a mountain lake in a grove of cottonwood trees about one and a half miles from the lodge. These charmers are each equipped with a kitchenette, fireplace, and queen-sized bed.

THE FACTS

Thirty-seven rooms, each with private bath; all with gas fireplaces; four with tubs for two. Restaurant, sporting goods store, swimming pool, two communal spas. Disabled access. Two-night minimum stay required during weekends; two-to-three-night minimum during holiday periods. Moderate to deluxe.

GETTING THERE

Freestone Inn is located on Highway 20, 1.5 miles northwest of Mazama. Weather permitting, inn is accessible via Highway 20 north of Seattle. When Highway 20 is closed, inn is accessed via Stevens Pass (Highway 2) or Snoqualmie Pass (Interstate 90). Driving time from Seattle ranges from four to five hours.

FREESTONE INN
31 Early Winters Drive
Mazama, WA 98833
Telephone: (509) 996-3906;
toll-free: (800) 639-3809
Web site: www.freestoneinn.com

FREESTONE INN

In addition to affording us an opportunity to update readers on changes in rates and rooms, revisions of this book give us a chance to share the occasional new Northwest discovery. We eagerly anticipated this third edition and the chance to introduce travelers to this mountain retreat, which represents everything we expect from a romantic getaway. Although Freestone Inn was but a gleam in the eyes of the owners when we first set out to identify the Northwest's most romantic getaways, it's now firmly established on our list of don't-miss destinations.

The warm and welcoming Freestone Inn is set on part of an old ranch property in beautiful Methow Valley, just northwest of Winthrop along the North Cascades Scenic Highway. The stone-, ironwork-, and timber-infused great room serves as an inviting guest destination, as does a spacious spa overlooking Freestone Lake. The lodge's lakeview restaurant is romantic and highly rated.

Recreation spans the seasons, and includes a trail system for mountain biking, hiking, horseback riding, and cross-country skiing. There's also ice skating on the lake during winter and a helicopter skiing service that's based at the inn.

ROOMS FOR ROMANCE

The lion's share of rooms are found in the main inn. These are nicely appointed, with comfortable chairs, attractive wall-mounted iron sconces, and king-sized beds. Each room in the inn also offers a gas fireplace and either a deck or a balcony. All have stunning views of Freestone Lake and the Cascades, which serve as a dramatic backdrop. A number of the rooms have vaulted ceilings.

Also on the property are two luxurious lakeside lodges, each with two or three bedrooms, a kitchen, and a living room. In addition, more than a dozen cabins, many of them dating back to the early days of the ranch, are available to those preferring more space and privacy.

THE FACTS

Fifteen rooms, each with private bath. Complimentary full breakfast served at tables for two or delivered to your room. Complimentary fresh fruit basket provided in your room. Disabled access. No minimum night stay requirement. Moderate.

GETTING THERE

From Seattle (250 miles), follow Highways 90 and 82 to Pasco. From Pasco, take Highway 124 east to Wallsburg. Follow Highway 12 to Dayton. Hotel is on Main Street. From Portland (210 miles), follow Highway 80 and Highway 730 to Walla Walla. Take Highway 12 to Dayton.

WEINHARD HOTEL
235 East Main Street
Dayton, WA 99328
Telephone: (509) 382-4032
Web site: www.weinhard.com

Okay, we may have stretched the boundaries of "Pacific Northwest" by including a Southeastern Washington destination. However, we doubt our readers will quibble over a technicality, especially after a visit to this Old West charmer.

Recommended by Washingtonians Alex and Susan Hayden, who respectively photographed and coordinated photography for this third edition of *Weekends for Two in the Pacific Northwest,* the Weinhard is a destination sure to be enjoyed by folks who enjoy history and Victoriana.

The Weinhard building, with its authentic brick facade, is a genuine antique, built by early Dayton settler Jacob Weinhard who came to town to open a brewery and malt house. He built this structure in 1890 to house the Weinhard Saloon and Lodge Hall. Despite many incarnations over the years, the building's heart and soul endure. Today, it's a living testament to life on the road in the early years of Eastern Washington— along with a healthy dose of modern-day comforts.

ROOMS FOR ROMANCE

The inn's fifteen rooms, created in 1994, are thankfully more spacious than the cramped quarters of early days, but the furnishings are true to the era. Ornate beds and armoires, some dating from the 1830s, grace the guest rooms. The bathrooms are modern, featuring tub-and-shower combinations with plenty of hot water. The rooms also feature other contemporary touches such as telephones and computer modems.

For a romantic getaway the likes of which early Dayton residents couldn't have imagined, our top pick is room 10 (mid $100 range), a second-floor room furnished with a queen-sized bed and a spa tub for two. This is the hotel's most expensive accommodation.

Another good choice is room 15 (around $100), which has a queen-sized bed and French doors that open to a balcony.

At the time of our travels, most rooms at the Weinhard were being offered for around $100 or less, making this a perfect destination for romantics on a budget. Inquire about romantic-getaway and other packages when making a reservation.

DAYTIME DIVERSIONS

In PORT TOWNSEND, ask your innkeeper about the one-hour walking tour of the village, browse the shops along Water Street, or tour a few of the restored Victorian homes open to visitors in the uptown area, where our two recommended inns are located. The Jefferson County Historical Museum is at Water and Madison Streets.

For more than a decade, the Wooden Boat Foundation has sponsored the popular Wooden Boat Festival in September. You can expect to see more than one hundred classic vessels ranging in length from eight to one hundred feet.

After seeing quaint Port Townsend, relax with your favorite refreshment at the Town Tavern, a hundred-year-old building on Water Street.

In SEATTLE, the freshest fish, juicy Washington fruits, sweet baked goods, antique clothing, and local handicrafts abound at the landmark Pike Place Market (First and Pike Streets). Inside the multilevel seven-acre marketplace, interesting twists and turns reveal unusual specialty shops that sell everything from vintage clothing to contemporary art. It's a must-see for visitors.

Pioneer Square (between Cherry and Jackson Streets), a short walk from the Alexis Hotel down First Avenue, offers a taste of early Seattle, with classic old buildings and lovely trees. In addition to eateries and shops, the square boasts more than two dozen art galleries.

Other local attractions include the ever-popular observation deck on the Space Needle (Fifth Avenue at Broad Street) for a view of the city and the Sound, the Seattle Aquarium (Pier 59), Woodland Park Zoo (between Fiftieth and Fifty-ninth Streets), and the Seattle Art Museum (First Avenue).

On WHIDBEY ISLAND, the village of Langley has numerous shops and galleries, as well as a movie theater. There's also a Scottish-style nine-hole golf course nearby. Whidbey's Greenbank Loganberry Farm offers self-guided tours and a tasting bar.

Orcas Aerodrome, operating out of the Eastsound Airport on ORCAS ISLAND, offers scenic biplane flights over the San Juan Islands. Bicycles, mopeds, and kayaks may also be rented on the island. On a clear day, Mount Constitution in Moran State Park offers romantic sunset vistas and unforgettable views of the islands. The park's Cascade Falls also makes for a romantic setting. And there's a nine-hole golf course on Orcas Island.

FERRY INFORMATION

For ferry schedules and information, call Washington State Ferries at (800) 843-3779, or log on to www.wsdot.wa.gov/ferries/.

TABLES FOR TWO

In LANGLEY, we recommend the Inn at Langley (dinner served Friday and Saturday), Cafe Langley (Greek/Mediterranean cuisine), the Star Bistro (burgers to seafood), and Francisco's Italian Restaurant. All are on First Street in downtown Langley.

In FRIDAY HARBOR, Maloula's serves Mediterranean and Middle Eastern cuisine on a harbor-view deck.

On ORCAS ISLAND, Christina's in Eastsound is considered to be among the best seafood restaurants in the San Juan Islands. Also recommended is Sunflower Cafe.

In PORT ANGELES, our hosts recommended Toga's and Bella Italia. Willcox House guests needn't leave the inn for a fine fixed-price meal.

Our PORT TOWNSEND innkeepers recommended the following restaurants: Fountain Cafe (Washington at Taylor Streets), an eight-table bistro serving pastas and cafe cuisine; Lanza's (on Lawrence in the uptown area), an informal Italian restaurant; Silverwater (on Quincy Street behind Town Tavern) for Northwestern cuisine; and Khularb Thai (Adams near Washington Street).

In SEATTLE, Metropolitan Grill on Second Avenue, and Andaluca on Olive Way score high on the list of this city's favorite romantic restaurants. Also recommended are Canlis, Wild Ginger, Il Bistro, and Adriatica.

While not the most intimate of settings, Tillicum Village on BLAKE ISLAND is a popular dinner destination, primarily because of the salmon smoked over an open fire. Ferries leave for Tillicum Village from Piers 55 and 56.

THE PUGET SOUND REGION

THE FACTS

Five rooms, each with private bath, spa tub for two, private patio, videocassette and compact disc players, and gas fireplace. Complimentary full breakfast served at tables for six. Disabled access. No multinight stay requirement. Moderate to expensive.

GETTING THERE

The inn is two hours from Seattle via Bainbridge Island ferry. From Seattle and Sea-Tac Airport, follow Interstate 5 north to Seattle waterfront and Bainbridge Island ferry. From the ferry, follow Highway 305 to Highway 3, to Highway 104, and to Highway 101 around Sequim. Drive approximately 5 miles past Sequim Avenue exit and turn right onto Kitchen-Dick Road (sign for Dungeness Wildlife Refuge). Drive 1.5 miles to Old Olympic Highway and turn left. Follow to Matson Road and turn right. Follow for a half-mile to Finn Hall Road and turn left. Follow approximately 1 mile to inn's driveway on right.

COLETTE'S BED AND BREAKFAST
339 Finn Hall Road
Port Angeles, WA 98362
Telephone: (360) 457-9197
Web site: www.colettes.com

COLETTE'S BED AND BREAKFAST

With a few exceptions, we can make a fairly accurate assumption about the romance quotient of an inn based on the driving directions. Generally speaking, our best discoveries are often the hardest to find. This lovely waterfront estate, set between the Olympic Mountains and the broad sweep of the Strait of Juan de Fuca, is one of those off-the-beaten-track gems.

Colette's ten acres consist of lush forest land, lawns, and gardens. Guests share the grounds with the occasional visiting deer, fox, and eagle. The daytime water vistas are magnificent; at the end of the day, sunsets give way to the shimmering lights of romantic Victoria just across the strait.

ROOMS FOR ROMANCE

The Iris Suite (low $200 range) consists of the west wing of the main house. Here a cushy love seat sits next to a fireplace at the foot of a king-sized iron bed, which commands a glorious water view through a huge window. The luxurious bathroom has a spa tub for two set under a garden-view window.

The Lavender and Azalea Suites (high $100 range) are found in the east wing of the main house. In Lavender, the king-sized bed is flanked on one side by a dual-sided gas fireplace, and on the other by a wall of windows revealing the lush grounds and the water. The other side of the fireplace faces the bathroom, a romantic retreat unto itself, featuring a spa tub for two set in a windowed corner.

Arguably the inn's most romantic accommodation, the Spruce Suite (mid $200 range) is situated in the adjacent Forest House. The suite is furnished with a four-poster bed, a gas fireplace, and a love seat placed before view windows. Outside is your own private water-view patio.

The Cedar Suite, which is styled in a similar fashion, is also a romantic favorite.

Eight rooms, each with private bath. No telephone or television in guest rooms. Game room equipped with billiard table, woodburning stove, and television and videocassette player. Complimentary multicourse breakfast served at communal table. Complimentary refreshments served in evening. No disabled access. Moderate to expensive.

From Seattle and Sea-Tac Airport, follow Interstate 5 north to Seattle waterfront and Bainbridge Island ferry. From ferry, follow signs to Hood Canal Bridge. Cross bridge and continue on Highway 104 to Highway 19 (Beaver Valley Road) turnoff, and follow signs to Port Townsend. Just past first stoplight at Kearny, turn left up to bluff (Washington Street). Inn is at corner of Washington and Walker Streets.

OLD CONSULATE INN

Known among locals for generations as "the red Victorian on the hill," the Old Consulate Inn is one of the most exquisite examples of Queen Anne architecture you'll find in this region. It's also one of the most romantic of the myriad inns in this enchanting community.

ROOMS FOR ROMANCE

Entering our room, the Master Anniversary Suite (low $200 range), we felt as if we'd stepped into the pages of a Victorian romance novel. The entire water-view side of the second floor is given over to this suite decorated with coordinating wall coverings. The suite features a lace-canopied king-sized bed, crystal chandeliers, a woodburning stove, a round sitting alcove, and a fabulous chandelier-lit bathroom with a clawfoot bathtub.

The Tower Honeymoon Suite (around $200) is another Victorian masterpiece. Located on the third floor, the room, set under the eaves, offers a round sitting room in the turret, a wicker king-sized bed placed under a half-moon-shaped window, and a small private bathroom.

Parkside (mid $100 range) is a second-floor corner room that faces the front of the inn. Decorated in lavender and lace and Waverly-patterned fabric, this room features a king-sized bed that sits under a harem-style tent ceiling.

Outdoors, a large, glass-paneled bay-view gazebo matching the inn's porch houses a hot tub with back-massage and moving water jets.

Old Consulate Inn
313 Walker Street
Port Townsend, WA 98368
Telephone: (360) 385-6753;
toll-free: (800) 300-6753
Web site: www.oldconsulateinn.com

THE FACTS

Eight rooms, each with private bath; three with fireplaces; two with tubs for two. Multicourse breakfast included. No disabled access. Moderate to deluxe.

GETTING THERE

From Seattle and Sea-Tac Airport, follow Interstate 5 north to Seattle waterfront and Bainbridge Island ferry. From ferry, follow signs to Hood Canal Bridge. Cross bridge and continue on Highway 104 to Highway 19 (Beaver Valley Road) turnoff, and follow signs to Port Townsend. In Port Townsend follow Sims Way as it turns into Water Street through Old Port Townsend. Turn left on Monroe and continue up the hill. Turn left on Clay and follow to inn at corner of Quincy and Clay Streets.

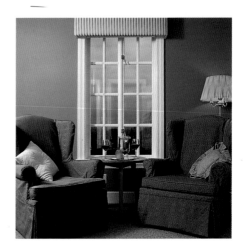

RAVENSCROFT INN

533 Quincy Street
Port Townsend, WA 98368
Telephone: (360) 385-2784
Web site: www.ravenscroftinn.com

RAVENSCROFT INN

In a town famous for old-fashioned Victorian inns, the Ravenscroft dares to be different in a most romantic way.

Constructed in contemporary times in a wood-sided and white-trimmed style that conjures images of the American South, the handsome inn is one of the most intriguing sites in this old Port Townsend neighborhood. A columned covered veranda runs the full width of the first and second levels, and dormer windows frame views of Port Townsend Bay and Indian and Marrowstone Islands.

This fresh, well-maintained inn tastefully combines modern comforts with antiques. The brightly painted public great room on the main floor includes a living area with a fireplace and an area with small dining tables next to the large open kitchen.

ROOMS FOR ROMANCE

Fireside (mid $100 range), a second-floor corner room, is equipped with a brick fireplace and a queen-sized four-poster bed. French doors open onto the covered veranda, and bay and mountain views are visible through the trees.

Down the hall is Bay (mid to upper $100 range), with a king-sized bed and French doors through which the bay and islands are visible.

On the third floor, we were particularly impressed with the eight-hundred-square-foot Mount Rainier Room (mid $200 range), with a king-sized bed and a dark green oval soaking tub for two. The room has a coffered ceiling, as well as dormer windows that offer views of the water. It also has access to a private balcony, and a private bath with a tiled shower and an antique pine sink.

The three most secluded rooms—Study, Quincy, and Bower—are partially below ground on what is called the garden level. These three rooms cost under $100.

The Admiralty Suite (around $200) is another romantic accommodation, with a queen-sized bed, a long clawfoot soaking tub, a view, and a gas fireplace.

THE FACTS

Five rooms, each with private bath; one with fireplace; one with spa tub for two. Amenities include extra-large towels, heated towel racks, bathrobes, down comforters, and basket of sundries in each room. Complete breakfast at private dining room table included; complimentary wine and cheese served every afternoon. Fixed-price multicourse dinners served by reservation; lunch is available to multinight guests. No disabled access. No minimum night stay requirement. Moderate to expensive.

GETTING THERE

Willcox House is located north of Holly and south of Seabeck on Tekiu Road. From Highway 3 in Bremerton, go west on Kitsap Way; fork left on Northlake Way; fork left on Seabeck Highway; left on Holly Road; left at stop sign on Seabeck-Holly Road; fork right on Old Holly Hill Road; and turn right at mailboxes on Tekiu Road and follow for 1.2 miles. Turn left at cabin to inn. Our best advice is to request a detailed map from Willcox House.

WILLCOX HOUSE COUNTRY INN
2390 Tekiu Road NW
Seabeck, WA 98380
Telephone: (360) 830-4492;
toll-free: (800) 725-9477
Web site: www.willcoxhouse.com

WILLCOX HOUSE COUNTRY INN

While some getaway-bound travelers find lengthy and detailed driving directions daunting, the two of us find them an exciting adventure. So we were especially intrigued upon receiving from Willcox House directions that resembled a pirate's treasure map.

At the end of a pleasant drive, Willcox House emerged as a treasure indeed. Originally the showplace Art Deco mansion of retired Marine Corps Col. Julian Willcox and his wife, Constance, the inn sits at the edge of Hood Canal, surrounded by extraordinary gardens. The Olympic Mountains loom in the distance.

In 1937, when much of the nation was still in the grips of the Great Depression, the Willcoxes invested a small fortune to create a modern showplace. They equipped the home with elegant nautically themed touches and paneled the exterior in an unusual synthetic red slate siding. The roof is made of copper.

Used in later years as a private school, the ten-thousand-square-foot home was restored and modernized by Cecilia and Phillip Hughes, who opened it as an inn in 1989.

ROOMS FOR ROMANCE

The premiere guest room is Constance's Room (upper $100 range), named after Mrs. Willcox. Equipped with a marble Art Deco fireplace and a king-sized bed, the room has an intriguing private bathroom with the toilet situated in a showerlike stall. The room's original built-in vanity is among the valuable vintage pieces preserved by the innkeepers.

Julian's Room (upper $100 range), decorated in a handsome English-country style, has a king-sized bed and a newer skylit bathroom equipped with a spa tub for two.

The namesake room of film star Clark Gable, one of the Willcox family's many famous guests, is equipped with a chaise longue and a balcony with garden-, water-, and mountain views. The nicely windowed room, offered in the upper $100 range, has a king-sized bed and a small bathroom with a shower.

In the Colonel's Room (mid $100 range), guests step up to the king-sized antique brass bed. The room has a view toward the water and a bathroom with a shower.

Guests making reservations should be aware that the Rose Garden Room (low $100 range) is entered through the inn's kitchen. Those wishing more privacy should request another room.

THE FACTS

Thirty rooms, each with private bath, sitting area, refrigerator, and compact disc player. Complimentary full breakfast served in dining room. Complimentary refreshments served every afternoon. Parking provided nearby at extra charge. Fitness center with indoor pool and separate lap pool. Disabled access. No minimum night stay requirement. Moderate to expensive.

GETTING THERE

From Interstate 5, take Seneca Street exit. Turn right on Sixth Avenue, turn left on Union, and turn left on First Avenue. Inn is on First Avenue between University and Seneca across street from Seattle Art Museum. Park in front of hotel to register.

INN AT HARBOR STEPS

Seattle has seen a flurry of boutique hotel openings since we first visited the city in search of romantic lodgings. Among our favorite of these intimate urban retreats is Inn at Harbor Steps, which occupies the lower floors of an upscale residential highrise on First Street in the arts and business district. The building adjoins the Harbor Steps, an outdoor plaza with broad steps leading to multiple levels of shops and restaurants.

Popular during the week among business travelers, the inn shifts gears a bit during the weekend, welcoming traveling couples intent on exploring the city. In addition to offering stylish and comfortable accommodations, the Inn at Harbor Steps is easily accessible to popular destinations like the Seattle Art Museum and Benaroya Hall. The famous and popular Pike Place Market is only three blocks away. Great restaurants are also within walking distance.

ROOMS FOR ROMANCE

Rooms here are generously sized for a city hotel, and are decorated in a handsome, traditional style with a mix of solids and patterns. Each has either a queen- or king-sized bed, and most have fireplaces and small sitting areas. Most rooms also feature a tiny balcony overlooking the adjacent Harbor Steps Park. Some rooms have spa tubs for two. Other niceties include wet bars, refrigerators, and phones with voice mail. Rooms with queen-sized beds are offered in the high $100 range, while rates for king-sized rooms with spa tubs are in the low $200 range.

More recently, the inn took over a number of luxury Harbor Steps condominium units to create ten spacious rooms, each of which has two queen-sized beds and a large balcony with outdoor seating. These are available in the low $200 range.

INN AT HARBOR STEPS

1221 First Avenue
Seattle, WA 98101
Telephone: (206) 748-0973;
toll-free: (888) 728-8910
Web site: www.foursisters.com

THE FACTS

Sixty-seven rooms, each with private bath. Guests have access to Bellevue Club services including indoor and out-door swimming pools, two fitness centers; tennis (indoor and outdoor), squash, and racquetball courts; indoor running track; day spa services; saunas; and aerobics studio. Restaurant, café, lounge, and bar. Disabled access. No minimum night stay requirement. Moderate to deluxe.

GETTING THERE

From Interstate 405, take S.E. Eighth Street exit (Exit 12) and turn west. Turn right on 114th Street; turn left on S.E. Sixth Street and follow to hotel on right.

BELLEVUE CLUB HOTEL

11200 S.E. Sixth Street
Bellevue, WA 98004
Telephone: (425) 454-4424;
toll-free: (800) 579-1110
Web site: www.bellevueclub.com

BELLEVUE CLUB HOTEL

A romantic getaway can take many forms. For some it might be a quiet weekend enjoying each other's company in a cozy room by a warming fire. Other couples enjoy a weekend together on the ski slopes or bike trails. The Bellevue Club Hotel is a destination for those of us who enjoy a healthy blend of being lazy and being active.

This wonderful full-service city resort is set on nearly ten acres in central Bellevue, only a fifteen-minute drive from downtown Seattle. Guests at the hotel have access to the myriad services of the private, upscale Bellevue Club. There are indoor and outdoor tennis courts, fitness centers, an indoor swimming pool, and day spa services, among other activities.

ROOMS FOR ROMANCE

The guest rooms are luxuriously furnished, and feature marble and limestone bathrooms with glass-enclosed showers and deep soaking tubs, cherry-wood furniture, in-room movie systems, twice-daily cleaning service, and twenty-four-hour room service. Most have king-sized beds.

The lowest priced accommodations are the Deluxe Rooms, offered in the mid $200 range and featuring private balconies with views of the tennis courts, gardens, or courtyard fountain.

The Premiere Rooms (mid $200 range) are bigger, and have either larger balconies, oversized bathrooms, or fireplaces. The Club Rooms (around $300), which are surrounded by gardens, boast twelve-foot ceilings and private terra-cotta patios. Club Room guests also receive a complimentary continental breakfast. The hotel also offers luxury suites priced in the upper $500 range.

Hotel guests have access to the club's private restaurant. Ask about weekend romance and spa packages when you call for reservations. At the time of our travels, the hotel was offering greatly reduced weekend rates.

THE FACTS

Eighty-six rooms, each with private bath, soaking tub for two, fireplace, compact disc and DVD player, morning paper, French press coffeemaker, and high-speed Internet access. Complimentary continental breakfast. Library, fitness center, and day spa. Two restaurants. Disabled access. Two-night minimum stay required during weekends. Expensive to deluxe.

GETTING THERE

From Highway 405 northbound, take Exit 20b (Exit 20 if traveling south) and turn right onto N.E. 124th Street. Drive to fourth stoplight and turn left onto 132nd Avenue N.E. Follow for 1.3 miles and turn right at the stop sign onto N.E. 143rd Place (to Woodinville). Follow to N.E. 145th Street and drive straight past Columbia Winery and Château Ste. Michelle Winery. Lodge is immediately past Redhook Brewery on left.

WILLOWS LODGE

What could be more romantic than a day in Washington's wine country? How about two days in the wine country and a night next door to two of the state's best wineries and one of Washington's preeminent breweries? New in 2000, Willows Lodge is the perfect luxury destination for lovers of food and drink as well as lovers of each other.

Sleek, stylish, rich, contemporary, traditional, sophisticated, playful—all these diverse descriptions combine to describe Willows Lodge, one of the Northwest's most romantic getaway experiences. From the soaring lobby area to the guest rooms, the lodge exudes quality. The timbers used throughout the buildings were recycled from the Port of Portland, and they give the lodge a rich and rustic look. The guest room tables are recycled slate pool tabletops from Canadian saloons. The beds are the best that money can buy, and the bedding is of the highest quality. The sinks are made of Mexican marble, the art is original, and the in-room refrigerators are noiseless.

The lodge was laid out so that most of the guest rooms face gardens featuring conifers, flowering trees, Japanese maples, large stones, and running water. Native plantings flow from the lodge to the edge of the adjacent Sammamish River. There's a hidden courtyard with a hydrotherapy pool and an Asian-inspired garden. There are also a fitness center and a day spa on-site.

ROOMS FOR ROMANCE

The guest rooms are classified as "nice," "nicer," and "nicest." All have large-screen televisions and DVD and compact disc players, stone-trimmed gas fireplaces, desks, and luxurious bathrooms whose soaking tubs for two have a clear sight line to a window, a fireplace, and a television. Guests also have access to compact disc and DVD libraries.

The rooms in the "nice" category (mid $200 range) face parking areas. "Nicer" rooms (upper $200 range) have more pleasant views. The "nicest" rooms (low $300 range) have all the above features, in addition to jetted spa tubs and heated towel warmers. Spacious suites are also offered from the mid $300 range to the mid $700 range.

WILLOWS LODGE

14580 N.E. 145th Street
Woodinville, WA 98072
Telephone: (425) 424-3900;
toll-free: (877) 424-3930
Web site: www.willowslodge.com

WILD IRIS INN

121 Maple Avenue (P.O. Box 696)
La Conner, WA 98257
Telephone: (360) 466-1400
Web site: www.wildiris.com

THE FACTS

Nineteen rooms and suites, each with private bath; suites furnished with gas fireplaces and spa tubs for two. Complimentary full breakfast served at tables for two or delivered to your room. Restaurant serving weekend dinners. Disabled access. No minimum night stay requirement. Moderate.

GETTING THERE

From Interstate 5, take Burlington exit (number 230) to Highway 20 west, and follow signs to La Conner. Turn left on Maple Avenue and follow for a half-block to inn on left.

WILD IRIS INN

The quaint waterside artist colony of La Conner is a perfect destination for Seattle-area residents who are in need of a romantic refresher but don't want to invest in hours on the road. It's also a great place to spend a night or two if you're on your way to other Puget Sound destinations.

The Wild Iris is a contemporary Victorian-style inn that, for such a relatively small property, manages to pack a number of romantic amenities into its nineteen accommodations. We also found it to be a comparative bargain, given its list of features.

ROOMS FOR ROMANCE

For a romantic getaway, we recommend one of the King or Queen Suites. The King Suites (upper $100 range) are the most lavish, offering king-sized beds, fireplaces, bathrooms with showers, in-room spa tubs for two, and spacious outdoor decks with nice views. Our favorite is room 105, the Cloud Room, whose centerpiece is a pretty fireplace above which is placed a wall-mounted television. This combination is flanked by two white columns. There's an adjacent spa tub for two set under a window.

The Queen Suites come with either indoor or outdoor spa tubs for two; the choice is yours. Three with private outdoor deck-mounted spa tubs are offered in the mid $100 range. They also have fireplaces and bathrooms with showers.

If the two of you prefer the indoors, we recommend one of the six suites with queen-sized beds, fireplaces, and indoor spa tubs (upper $100 range). These also have private outdoor balconies.

CLIFF HOUSE AND THE COTTAGE
727 Windmill Drive
Freeland, WA 98249
Telephone: (360) 331-1566
Web site: www.cliffhouse.net

THE FACTS

Cliff House: two bedrooms and two and a half baths, one with a single spa tub; full kitchen, fireplace, outdoor spa, deck, television/videocassette player, and compact disc sound system. Complimentary continental breakfast provided. No disabled access. Two-night minimum stay typically required. Deluxe. Cottage: one bedroom and one bath, fireplace, television and videocassette player, and deck. Complimentary continental breakfast provided. No disabled access. No minimum night stay requirement. Moderate to expensive.

GETTING THERE

From Clinton ferry terminal, follow Highway 525 north for about 10.5 miles to Bush Point Road. Turn left and drive 1.5 miles to Windmill Road and turn left. At Cliff House sign, turn right down winding drive to compound. For ferry schedules and information, call Washington State Ferries at (800) 843-3779, or log on to www.wsdot.wa.gov/ferries/.

CLIFF HOUSE AND THE COTTAGE

These two seductive hideaways, set on a cliff overlooking Admiralty Straits, represent a romantic hybrid of sorts: a cross between a vacation rental home and a bed-and-breakfast inn. Proprietors Peggy Moore and Walter O'Toole live in separate quarters, so guests have full use of the house or cottage. However, Peggy and Walter are nearby to offer tips on hiking, dining, and the like, and they also leave a large continental breakfast in the refrigerator for their guests. Guests can also walk down a stairway to a very private beach.

ROOMS FOR ROMANCE

Whether you choose the Cliff House or the cottage depends on whether you prefer spacious, contemporary, and expensive or small, rustic, and cozy.

Cliff House (high $400 range) is a stunning, architectural-award-winning two-bedroom home built around an atrium. A massive stone fireplace separates the dining room from a sunken living area equipped with a large couch, a compact disc player with 150 compact discs, and a videocassette player with hundreds of videos. The interior floors are made of gleaming slate. Outside is a large deck with a spa and a hammock.

The two bedrooms are located upstairs. The master bedroom features a king-sized bed and expansive windows that open to views of Puget Sound. The smaller bedroom, equipped with a full-sized, extra-long bed, offers a view of the forest.

While Cliff House can accommodate two couples for around $500, guests should be aware that both of the bedrooms are partially open to and visible from the lower living area. Consequently, it is not completely private.

A few hundred yards from the house is the very romantic cottage (high $100 range), a charming older structure that has been completely rebuilt and updated. Trimmed in pink and set amid native plants and trees, the cottage has knotty-pine walls, a full kitchen, an antique oak table and chairs, a fireplace, a window seat, and a queen-sized feather bed. Out back is a large deck facing the water, a hammock, and a tree house with chairs.

THE FACTS

Twenty-four rooms and two cottages, each with private bath, spa tub for two, water view, deck, woodburning fireplace, television, videocassette player, telephone, and refrigerator. Complimentary continental breakfast served each morning in country kitchen; dining room open weekends for dinner. Two-night minimum stay on weekends. Disabled access. Expensive to deluxe.

GETTING THERE

Ferry ride from Mukilteo to Whidbey Island takes less than an hour. From Clinton ferry terminal, follow Highway 525 north to Langley Road stoplight and turn right. Follow for about 3 miles into Langley. At first stop sign, take a right onto Cascade Avenue, which becomes First Street. Inn is at edge of village's business section, on right. For ferry schedules and information, call Washington State Ferries at (800) 843-3779, or log on to www.wsdot.wa.gov/ferries/

INN AT LANGLEY

To an unknowing passerby, the Inn at Langley might initially be mistaken for an upscale motel. Don't let first impressions fool you. A quick look at the soaring architecture of the beachside facade and a tour of one of the sublime guest rooms will reveal a contemporary romantic-getaway destination unrivaled in Washington's islands.

Although the sandy Saratoga Passage shoreline behind the inn is accessible for strolling, there is no swimming beach here.

ROOMS FOR ROMANCE

Unlike some inns, where the lion's share of attention is lavished on the exterior at the expense of creature comforts, the Inn at Langley spares no expense in creating top-of-the-line guest rooms, all of which are honeymoon quality.

The inn's twenty-four rooms, spread over four levels, all offer the same spectacular views of Saratoga Passage. Each is equipped with a fireplace, a queen-sized bed, and a large two-person spa tub placed under a window with a water view. The tubs, connected to large two-person showers, are discreetly positioned so as to encourage soaking with the blinds open. The rooms also have tiled private decks, although these are situated fairly close to each other.

All rooms have wool carpeting and are furnished with comfortable cedar chairs with striped cushions. Wide wooden blinds cover the expansive windows.

There are three levels of accommodations at the inn. The standard guest rooms, offered in the low $200 range, more than sufficiently met all our requirements for a special romantic weekend. The corner rooms—there are six of these—are a bit larger and are offered in the mid $200 range. The two suites (high $300 range) have separate bedrooms, and couches in the living areas.

Since our last visit, Inn at Langley has created two delightful cottages (mid $500 range) next door to the inn. The inn also offers day spa services.

Five-course dinners are served in the dining room on Friday and Saturday nights, and Sundays from May to September. Plan on spending around $200 per couple, including wine.

Whale watchers should note that gray whales cruise the Saratoga Passage during the spring to feed on ghost shrimp, and the inn's balconies are perfect places from which to watch the parade.

THE FACTS

Fifteen rooms, each with private bath with oversized shower, and fireplace; most with water views. Complimentary full breakfast served in dining room. Complimentary refreshments served in afternoon. Free bicycle rentals. Disabled access. No minimum night stay requirement. Moderate to expensive.

GETTING THERE

Ferry ride from Mukilteo to Whidbey Island takes less than an hour. From Clinton ferry terminal, follow Highway 525 north to Langley Road stoplight and turn right. Follow for about 3 miles into Langley. At first stop sign, take a right onto Cascade Avenue and follow to inn on left.

SARATOGA INN

Langley made an obviously favorable impression on the two of us, as we opted to include not one but two destinations overlooking the incredible Saratoga Passage. The addition of this casually elegant inn provides yet another option for Whidbey Island–bound romantic travelers.

This charming destination, known in its former incarnation as Harrison House Inn, is now part of the Four Sisters Inns group, which operates Seattle's Inn at Harbor Steps (see separate listing) and a number of other reliably romantic hideaways we've sampled in California.

Evoking images of New England, the inn sports an attractive shingled, white-trimmed, and gabled facade and a wraparound porch. It's also an intimate property, offering only fifteen guest rooms.

In the public area, an open fireplace separates the warm and inviting lobby from the dining room, where guests enjoy a full breakfast at tables for two.

ROOMS FOR ROMANCE

The richness and warmth of the public rooms extends to the guest rooms, styled in prints and plaids. Each of the inn's rooms has a fireplace, and most offer grand views of the Saratoga Passage. The bathrooms all feature oversized showers for two.

Our top picks for a romantic getaway are the deluxe and king-bedded rooms (around $200) on the second level. Among these are rooms 10 and 11, which are furnished with king-sized beds and large-screen TVs. Both have water and mountain views. Rooms 14 and 15 are second-floor deluxe rooms with queen-sized beds, large-screen TVs, town and water views, and private decks.

The inn's separate Carriage House Suite (high $200 range), a 650-square-foot self-contained romantic haven, has a kitchen and a sun deck, as well as a king-sized sleigh bed, a stone fireplace, and a bathroom with a cast-iron tub.

SARATOGA INN
201 Cascade Avenue (P.O. Box 428)
Langley, WA 98260
Telephone: (360) 221-5801;
toll-free: (800) 698-2910
Web site: www.foursisters.com

TURTLEBACK FARM INN

1981 Crow Valley Road
Eastsound, WA 98245
Telephone: (360) 376-4914;
toll-free: (800) 376-4914
Web site: www.turtlebackinn.com

THE FACTS

Eleven rooms, each with private bath; four with fireplaces. Complimentary full breakfast served in dining room and in some guest rooms. Complimentary refreshments also available. Disabled access. Two-night minimum stay from mid-June through mid-October and during most weekends and holiday periods. Moderate.

GETTING THERE

From Orcas ferry landing, follow Orcas Road for 2.8 miles. Take the first left turn and follow nearly 1 mile. Turn right on Crow Valley Road and drive 1.5 miles to inn on right. For ferry schedules and information, call Washington State Ferries at (800) 843-3779, or log on to www.wsdot.wa.gov/ferries/.

TURTLEBACK FARM INN

As our Orcas Island ferry disgorged its cargo of cars, we found ourselves traveling bumper-to-bumper along Orcas Road, the island's main thoroughfare. Turning left off the highway after a couple of miles, however, we left the traffic behind and headed out on a deserted side road and into Crow Valley.

It was in this serene valley that Bill and Susan Fletcher (Susan is the daughter of the late film star Buster Crabbe) discovered a decrepit 1800s-era dairy and farmhouse and painstakingly renovated it to create Turtleback Farm Inn.

Open since 1985, the inn has earned a solid reputation as a romantic place to spend a night off Orcas Island's well-beaten path but within easy reach of the principal village of Eastsound. Bill and Susan have created an environment that most guests can't wait to tell their friends about.

From the road, the green-and-white inn resembles a quaint, lovingly tended farmhouse. So true to style was the renovation that it's difficult to tell that the Fletchers have expanded the house considerably to accommodate seven guest rooms and seven private baths.

Still a working farm, Turtleback is home to a number of critters, including sheep, chickens, and Scottish Highland cows.

ROOMS FOR ROMANCE

The rooms feature warm-toned fir floors, patterned area rugs, and soft colors. All except one are equipped with clawfoot tubs with overhead showers. The 1920s-era pedestal sinks came from Victoria's Empress Hotel. Other accessories were rescued from the old Savoy Hotel in Seattle. Pieces from the Fletchers' extensive antique collection complete the furnishings.

This bucolic property also includes the Orchard House, a cedar-sided addition that houses the most romantic rooms (low $200 range). Each features a gas fireplace, a sitting area, a dining area, a refrigerator, a compact disc player, and a full bath with a clawfoot soaking tub and a large shower. Breakfast is served to these rooms.

With rates in the mid $100 range, Valley View and Meadow View are very special rooms. Valley View, a rear corner room, is furnished with a love seat, a queen-sized bed, and an antique Australian dresser. The room also has a small private deck looking east to Mount Constitution. Meadow View, with a queen-sized bed, also opens to a private deck overlooking a meadow that sweeps down behind the house.

Elm View, also offered in the mid $100 range, is a privately situated second-floor corner room. Elm View features a queen-sized bed and a sitting area, and there's an unusual floor-level window in the bathroom with a nice view.

A bargain at less than $100, the Nook is a small and cozy room with a double bed.

THE FACTS

Twenty-six cottages and suites, each with fireplace, video-cassette player, microwave, refrigerator, and compact disc player. Some with spa tubs for two. Complimentary continental breakfast served in lobby area. Swimming pool. Marina. Restaurant serves dinner nightly during summer season; Wednesday through Sunday during rest of year. Two-night minimum stay required during summer weekends and holiday periods. Expensive to deluxe.

GETTING THERE

Ferry ride from Anacortes to Orcas Island takes about an hour and a half. From ferry at Orcas Island, drive approximately 2.5 miles to Deer Harbor Road. Turn left and follow for 4.5 miles. Resort is on left. For ferry schedules and information, call Washington State Ferries at (800) 843-3779, or log on to www.wsdot.wa.gov/ferries/.

RESORT AT DEER HARBOR

A millennium metamorphosis transformed what started out as an apple farm into an enchanting waterside resort that we regard as the San Juan Islands' most romantic getaway destination.

As recently as the 1940s, this gorgeous property was planted with apple trees, and some of the orchard workers lived in tiny clapboard hillside cottages. Some of those bungalows, now bearing little resemblance to the modest dwellings of yesteryear, are part of the mix of cottages and suites that today make up the Resort at Deer Harbor.

This tidy enclave, set against a backdrop of trees and overlooking a sandy beach and Deer Harbor Marina, underwent a multi-million-dollar renovation at the turn of the new century. The resort owners clearly had traveling romantics in mind when they went to work on the eighteen freestanding cottages and collection of luxury suites.

ROOMS FOR ROMANCE

The apple pickers of the 1940s wouldn't recognize the resort's Historical Cottages today. These hideaways (high $100 range), which are among our favorite Deer Harbor rooms, boast microwaves, wood stoves, and private decks with outdoor spa tubs for two—and a view.

Also highly recommended are the Deluxe Cottages (mid $200 range), which hold king-sized beds, fireplaces, and luxurious bathrooms with spa tub for two. Another wonderful accommodation is the Garden Suite (mid $200 range), which has a king-sized bed, sitting room with fireplace, and a separate bedroom also with a fireplace. The Junior Suites (low $200 range), situated near the beach, have fireplaces and queen-sized beds.

The Deer Harbor Marina offers boat and bike rentals, as well as seasonal whale watching and kayak wildlife tours.

RESORT AT DEER HARBOR
31 Jack and Jill Lane (P.O. Box 200)
Deer Harbor, WA 98243
Telephone: (360) 376-4420
Web site: www.deerharbor.com

THE FACTS

Twenty rooms, each with private bath, gas fireplace, and tub for two. Complimentary continental breakfast served in dining room. Restaurant. Disabled access. Two-night minimum stay required during summer weekends and during holiday periods. Expensive to deluxe.

GETTING THERE

From Interstate 5, take Burlington/Anacortes–San Juan Ferry exit (exit 230), following Anacortes ferry signs. Ride to Friday Harbor aboard Washington State Ferry takes approximately one and a half hours. From ferry, follow traffic right on Front Street, which turns left up Spring Street. Turn right at First Street and right on West Street. Inn is at end of block. For ferry schedules and information, call Washington State Ferries at (800) 843-3779, or log on to www.wsdot.wa.gov/ferries/.

FRIDAY HARBOR HOUSE

The folks who brought you the romantic Inn at Langley (see separate listing) are also responsible for creating this equally upscale property, built a few years ago on a bluff overlooking the dramatic San Juan Channel, neighboring Orcas Island, and distant Mount Constitution.

Unlike the typical Victorian-style bed-and-breakfast inns that are so common to the villages and back roads of the San Juan Islands, Friday Harbor House resembles a stylish, contemporary villa, its striking facade combining white siding, copper panels, and cedar shingles.

In addition to offering twenty rooms furnished with features today's traveling romantics appreciate, this intimate inn also operates a highly rated water-view dining room that serves Northwest cuisine, drawing on ingredients from local waters and farms.

ROOMS FOR ROMANCE

Although the layout and size of the accommodations vary, all twenty of the inn's comfortable guest rooms have broad windows, gas fireplaces, remote-controlled stereo televisions, spa tubs for two (some with a view through the room and over the water), refrigerators, and videocassette players. Some also have tiny balconies. A few rooms do not have full water views; make sure you ask for a room in the main building with a waterfront vista. The corner rooms are the most coveted.

The rooms on the second and third floors are the most expensive. If you're visiting from late May through September, plan on spending in the mid to upper $200 range for a queen-bedded, harbor-view room. A luxurious third-floor suite is available for around $300. The inn's winter room rates start at under $200 per night.

FRIDAY HARBOR HOUSE
130 West Street (P.O. Box 1385)
Friday Harbor, WA 98250
Telephone: (360) 378-8455
Web site: www.fridayharborhouse.com

DAYTIME DIVERSIONS

Although you'll share the famous Butchart Gardens, twenty minutes from downtown VICTORIA, with busloads of international visitors, there are plenty of places within the fifty colorful acres of flowers, trees, fountains, and lawns to enjoy a private moment. It's a romantic must-see, especially during a warm summer evening. Sprawling Beacon Hill Park, another romantic destination, is within a short walk of Abigail's Hotel. A path winds along the wind-sculpted coastal bluffs adjacent to Dallas Road.

High tea at the palatial Empress Hotel is an elegant way to spend a late afternoon. The Royal British Columbia Museum, across the street from the Empress, houses impressive interpretive exhibits and magnificent collections of Canadiana. For a tour of the city, hop aboard one of the red double-decker buses in front of the Empress. Shopping along Government Street is another favorite pastime.

Craigdarroch Castle, which is open for tours, is within walking distance of Prior House and Fairholme Manor.

From your room at Sooke Harbour House, a brisk mile-long walk to the end of narrow Whiffen Spit and back will work up your appetite for the wonderful dinners served at the inn. Low tides in front of the Harbour House provide great opportunities for morning beachcombing. East Sooke Park is also a great daytime destination.

TABLES FOR TWO

In VICTORIA, the Herald Street Caffe (Herald Street near Government Street) is acknowledged by many innkeepers as one of the city's best restaurants. The Metropolitan Diner (Government Street near Herald Street) is also highly recommended, as is Camille's on Bastion Square. Join the convivial crowd at the popular Pagliacci's (Broad Street near Eaton Centre) for Italian fare. For a rich daytime dessert, visit bustling Murchie's on Government Street.

In SOOKE, you won't have to leave the grounds of Sooke Harbour House. The inn's restaurant, operated by Sinclair and Fredrique Philip, is among the most highly rated in all of Canada. The sight of white-uniformed cooking staff selecting fresh ingredients from the lush gardens outside your room is quite romantic and memorable.

Guests at the Aerie are treated to the acclaimed dining room with cuisine and views to die for.

FERRY INFORMATION

For Vancouver Island–bound ferry schedules, call BC Ferries at (250) 386-3431 or log onto www.bcferries.bc.ca.

VANCOUVER ISLAND, BRITISH COLUMBIA

THE FACTS

Six rooms, each with private bath, fireplace, and refrigerator stocked with complimentary drinks. Complimentary multicourse breakfast served in dining room or your room. High tea with home-baked specialties served daily. No disabled access. Moderate to deluxe.

GETTING THERE

From southbound Highway 17/Blanshard Avenue in downtown Victoria, turn left on Fort Street. Drive up hill approximately 1 mile to Saint Charles and turn right. Drive half-mile to inn on right.

PRIOR HOUSE BED AND BREAKFAST INN
620 Saint Charles
Victoria, BC V8S 3N7
Canada
Telephone: (250) 592-8847;
toll-free: (877) 924-3300
Web site: www.priorhouse.com

PRIOR HOUSE BED AND BREAKFAST INN

While the majority of visitors to Victoria spend their days and nights in the bustling downtown district, there are other romantic sides to this enchanting city.

One of our favorites is Rockland, the prestigious and quiet neighborhood just minutes from downtown, where Victoria's old money built grand homes at the turn of the century. Among these landmark residences is Prior House, constructed in 1912 for the King of England's representative to British Columbia.

Set adjacent to the expansive grounds of Government House, the mansion is now a stunningly renovated inn that treats visitors to a taste of the good life enjoyed by early Victorian islanders.

ROOMS FOR ROMANCE

The diversity of the inn's six elegant accommodations will ensure that you visit at least a half dozen times to fully savor the romance of this luxurious destination. Our two favorites—The Lieutenant Governor's and Windsor—are aptly described as "celebration suites." The Lieutenant Governor's Suite (around $300) is a spacious second floor hideaway furnished with European antiques and lit by crystal chandeliers. Guests are also treated to a king-sized bed, a fireplace, a private balcony, and a palatial gilded bathroom fit for royalty. It features a mirrored ceiling, swan-styled fixtures and a decadent spa tub for two.

Occupying the entire third floor, the private Windsor Penthouse (around $300) offers the best of the indoors and outdoors. The bedroom, which has two queen-sized beds, opens to a comfortable sitting room with a fireplace. The Windsor also boasts a marble shower and a marble whirlpool tub placed under a skylight. French doors open from the sitting room to a private deck offering views of the grounds, the ocean, and the Olympic Peninsula.

The inn's other rooms carry peak weekend rates in the low $200 range. Among these is the enchanting Hobbit, reached via a round-topped door set in a vine-covered stone wall. Inside is a beautiful bedroom with a canopied queen-size bed and a fireplace. The bathroom has a large spa tub and a separate shower. This room also has a private patio.

The Royal View Suite is a lovely, corner room with a small deck and a handsome canopied queen-size bed placed adjacent to a sitting area and a bay window. The bathroom is a destination unto itself and boasts a fireplace and a large spa tub with a view.

THE FACTS

Six rooms, each with private bath. Complimentary full breakfast served at tables for two or more or delivered to your room. No disabled access. Two-night minimum stay required during weekends and holiday periods. Moderate to deluxe.

GETTING THERE

From Highway 17/Blanshard Avenue in downtown Victoria, turn left on Fort Street and follow to St. Charles Street. Turn right and follow to Rockland Avenue. Turn right and make an immediate left onto Rockland Place.

FAIRHOLME MANOR
638 Rockland Place
Victoria, BC V8S 3R2
Canada
Telephone: (250) 598-3240
Web site: www.fairholmemanor.com

For generations, the pricey real estate of Victoria's affluent Rockland district could only be savored by a wealthy few of the city's elite. Fortunately for the rest of us, a handful of these grand mansions have in recent years begun to open their doors as luxurious inns. Among the newest mansion-turned-inns is Fairholme Manor, located next door to Government House and a stone's throw from Prior House, the previously featured property.

Welcoming guests only since 1999, this stately century-old Italianate manse commands a lush acre of lawns and gardens and a lovely view of trees, water, and mountains. It's everything you'd expect of an estate whose neighboring property is the official residence of British Columbia's lieutenant governor.

ROOMS FOR ROMANCE

Our favorite is the spacious Olympic Grand Suite (around $300), a resplendent space with cushy white overstuffed chairs and couch, an eleven-foot-high ceiling, large bay windows, a table and chairs, a sunroom, a fireplace, and a lavish bathroom with a soaking tub big enough for two. Guests here also enjoy a private deck with panoramic ocean- and mountain views. In 2002, Fairholme Manor created a new grand suite styled in a manner similar to the Olympic Grand.

Another room fit for special occasions is the Rose Garden Suite (upper $200 range). A beautiful duvet-covered bed dominates this room, which also features a fireplace and a charming bay-windowed seating area furnished with two overstuffed chairs. A French door opens to a private ocean-view deck. The bathroom has a large soaking tub, and there's also a kitchen with an eating nook overlooking the garden.

Equally impressive is the Penthouse Suite (mid $200 range), which boasts a full ocean- and mountain view. There's a heavenly living room with white overstuffed furniture, expansive windows, an eating nook, and a gas fireplace. The bedroom, whose centerpiece is a queen-sized sleigh bed, overlooks the Government House garden. The bathroom has a spa tub for two.

ABIGAIL'S HOTEL
906 McClure Street
Victoria, BC V8V 3E7
Canada
Telephone: (250) 388-5363;
toll-free: (800) 561-6565
Web site: www.abigailshotel.com

THE FACTS

Twenty-three rooms, each with private bath, some with deep soaking or spa tubs for two; more than half with woodburning fireplaces. All beds have goose-down comforters, and all rooms have fresh flowers. Complimentary full breakfast served in dining room or delivered to your room with advance notice. Complimentary refreshments served every afternoon in library. No disabled access. Expensive to deluxe.

GETTING THERE

From Highway 17/Blanshard Avenue in downtown Victoria, turn left on Humboldt Street, drive two blocks and turn left on Vancouver Street. After three and a half blocks, turn left on McClure Street to hotel at end of cul-de-sac.

Struck immediately by the storybook facade of this enchanting inn, we were sold even before we set foot in the door. A night here simply confirmed our attraction.

Located at the end of a quiet cul-de-sac in a mature neighborhood chockablock with apartment houses, this charming inn, with its geometric angles and half-timbered facade, offers instant romantic appeal. While the Tudor-style cement stucco exterior is original, the former apartment building was essentially gutted to create an impressive collection of guest rooms, each with a private bath. The hotel's name was taken from a famous sculpture by Rodin of a young woman with flowers in her hat.

The inn's first level houses a well-stocked library, a kitchen, and a sunny dining room in which a full breakfast is served. Guest rooms are spread primarily among the three upper floors, which are served only by stairs since Abigail's does not have an elevator. Consequently, using the stairs to get to and from the second-through-fourth-floor guest rooms may be difficult for the physically challenged. However, the trek up the stairs does provide a great excuse for relaxing in your room.

ROOMS FOR ROMANCE

We recommend rooms that face the front of the property; the rear rooms face an apartment building on the other side of the parking area.

Our room for the night, the luxurious Canterbury Bell (low $300 Canadian range), sat high on the top level, occupying a sunny, front-facing corner. Full of interesting angles and nooks, the room held two comfy wing chairs set before an Italian-marble woodburning fireplace. We also enjoyed a fireplace view from the king-sized bed, dressed in William Morris prints and placed under a canopied gable. A cushioned wicker chaise longue sat at the foot of the bed. The room's gabled bathroom, offering a peek of the Olympic Peninsula, was opulently equipped with a decadent Italian-marble spa tub for two, along with a pedestal sink and a bidet. The tub had a hand-held shower attachment. The Orchid Room at the opposite end of the third floor is similarly styled.

The Country Rooms (low $200 Canadian) have either one queen or two double beds and offer soaking tubs. The Fireplace and Rose Rooms (high $200 Canadian range) have queen-sized beds, woodburning fireplaces (the Rose Room has a double-sided fireplace), and either spas or deep soaking tubs.

Since our last visit, Abigail's has added six additional upscale Coach House rooms (low to mid $300 Canadian range). These are the ultimate romantic hideaways, offering four-poster king-sized beds, leather love seats, and spectacular marble bathrooms with spa tubs.

THE FACTS

Six rooms, each with private bath, spa tub for two, compact disc player, fresh flowers, and fireplace. Telephone located in parlor. Guests may choose a complimentary continental or full gourmet champagne breakfast delivered to their room. No disabled access. Expensive to deluxe.

GETTING THERE

From Highway 17/Blanshard Avenue in downtown Victoria, turn left on Humboldt Street and drive one block to corner of Quadra and Humboldt Streets.

HUMBOLDT HOUSE
867 Humboldt Street
Victoria, BC V8V 2Z6
Canada
Telephone: (250) 383-0152;
toll-free: (888) 383-0327
Web site: www.humboldthouse.com

HUMBOLDT HOUSE

For couples who want to savor peace and quiet in an ultraromantic setting, there is no better place than Humboldt House. Situated down the street from the quaint Beaconsfield Hotel and next to the old Saint Anne's Academy on a quiet, tree-lined street, this slender yellow-and-white Victorian resembles a comfortable family home.

ROOMS FOR ROMANCE

Edward's Room (high $200 Canadian range) faces front and offers a glimpse of the towers of the famous Empress Hotel. The room contains a handsome marble fireplace with a wood mantel and a spa tub for two draped in rich taffeta and crowned with a gingerbread-trimmed canopy.

Our hideaway for a night was the exotic and romantic Oriental Room (around $300 Canadian), with Chinese red walls and green carpet. In it, two hulking iron lions presided over the fireplace, and wooden shutters covered the windows. A sexy, ornately carved Oriental lamp (on a dimmer switch) cast a soft, romantic light over the room. Gazing out the window from the king-sized bed, we could see the spires of the grand old Empress Hotel in the distance.

A couple of steps above the bedroom, behind a lattice screen, sat a sunken, black spa tub for two. A sliding screen covered an orchard-view window just above the tub.

The spacious Gazebo Room (low $300 Canadian range) commands a pretty side view of the adjacent Saint Anne's Academy grounds. The room features a canopied queen-sized bed, a fireplace trimmed with green marble and cedar, a wicker love seat, and a step-up tub for two set in terra-cotta tile.

There is a comfortable parlor with a fireplace and a library just inside the front door, but most guests prefer the privacy of their own rooms. You'll not even have to open the door for breakfast, as meals are placed each morning in mailbox nooks in each room.

While romance comes easy in these sensuous rooms, showers can be tricky in the four rooms where the large tubs are equipped with hand-held spray attachments. You may agree with us that it works best to lend each other a helping hand.

THE FACTS

Twenty-eight rooms, each with private bath, bathrobe, ocean-view patio or balcony, woodburning fireplace, fresh flowers, and fruit; most have spa tubs for two. Complimentary full breakfast and lunch served. All rooms have wet bars stocked with complimentary teas, coffee, and cookies. Gourmet restaurant. Disabled access. Moderate to deluxe.

GETTING THERE

From Highway 1 north of Victoria, take Sooke/Colwood turnoff (Highway 14) and follow highway west to Sooke. Approximately 1 mile past Sooke traffic light, turn left on Whiffen Spit Road and follow to inn. Sooke Harbour House is 23 miles west of Victoria. Drive takes approximately forty minutes.

Sooke Harbour House

1528 Whiffen Spit Road
Sooke, BC V0S 1N0
Canada
Telephone: (250) 642-3421
Web site: www.sookeharbourhouse.com

SOOKE HARBOUR HOUSE

For many of us, a glorious meal, peace and quiet, and a room with a view are the key ingredients of a truly memorable romantic getaway. Since they're rarely found in the same place, it's exciting to discover a destination that nourishes both body and soul.

Restaurateurs Sinclair and Fredrique Philip could have rested on their laurels after establishing what most agree is one of the finest dining establishments in Canada. However, they went the extra kilometer by also becoming innkeepers, creating a small inn that has grown since our first visit to twenty-eight romantic water-view accommodations.

The resort traces its origin to the little 1930s-era farmhouse that serves as its centerpiece. Although a restaurant for many years, it took the Philips to put it on the map. One of the world's leading experts on edible flowers and herbs and a driving force in defining British Columbia's Northwest cuisine, Sinclair harvests vegetables, herbs, and flowers from his own backyard. Fish are taken from local waters, and meats and eggs are purchased from nearby farms.

ROOMS FOR ROMANCE

Although not quite as private as those in the newer additions, the three upstairs guest rooms in the farmhouse are our favorites. The Blue Heron commands the best view of the strait and the distant Olympic Mountains. In the fir-paneled sitting area is a spa tub for two set before a beachstone fireplace. On the upper level are a king-sized bed and wet bar. The room also has a large private deck.

In Sea Song, a king-sized bed sits on a raised fir floor, next to a large spa tub for two with a water view. Guests step down to the sitting area, equipped with a slate fireplace and a white couch. French doors open to a large balcony that overlooks the water. The skylit bathroom has an antique washbasin and a separate shower.

Room 1, also in the farmhouse, features a king-sized bed, a fireplace, and a spa tub for two romantically illuminated by a chandelier on a dimmer switch. The three farmhouse rooms are offered in the low $200 to around $400 Canadian range.

THE FACTS

Twenty-nine rooms, each with private bath; eighteen with gas or woodburning fireplaces; twenty-two with tubs for two. Complimentary full breakfast served in restaurant. Indoor swimming pool, hot tub, day spa, tennis courts, restaurant, and bar. No disabled access. Expensive to deluxe.

GETTING THERE

From Highway 1, approximately 25 miles north of Victoria, exit on Whittaker Road (Spectacle Lake turnoff). Turn right on Ebedora Lane and follow for approximately 1 mile to inn. Inquire about train service from Victoria.

THE AERIE

600 Ebedora Lane (P.O. Box 108)
Malahat, BC V0R 2L0
Canada
Telephone: (250) 743-7115;
toll-free: (800) 518-1933
Web site: www.aerie.bc.ca

Ah, to be in love and living in Victoria. At each compass point from the city are some of the Pacific Coast's most romantic destinations, and all are within easy reach. To the west, there's Sooke Harbour House; just a ferry boat ride south are the sublime hideaways of the lush Olympic Peninsula; and east are the enchanting San Juans. Our personal favorite, a half-hour drive north, is the Aerie. At no other place in the Pacific Northwest will your romantic yearnings be so completely indulged than on this sensuous summit.

Inspired by the similarities between this idyllic setting and her native Austria, proprietor Maria Schuster set about building a world-class inn reminiscent of those found in Europe. The glistening white Mediterranean-style structure set against the hillside is visible for miles.

If you think the inn makes for an impressive sight from the road below, just wait until you first gaze out through the window of one of the guest rooms. The sight of the majestic Finlayson Arm waterway winding through mountains cloaked in green will make your knees weak. Combine the view and decor with a romantic partner, and you may not be able to summon the strength to leave.

All guests of the Aerie have access to an indoor pool, a communal hot tub, and tennis courts. Three public golf courses are within a twenty-minute drive. The inn also has a day spa that offers massages for couples, facials, body relaxation treatments, and hair care.

ROOMS FOR ROMANCE

As you might expect, rates for the Aerie's nicer suites are as lofty as its location. For example, the decadent multilevel Aerie Suite, with large private decks, an oversized spa tub for two, and a king-sized four-poster bed, commands around $500 Canadian per night during peak season, which generally runs from July through early September. The Master Suites, featuring king-sized beds, spa tubs, and covered private balconies, are priced in the low $400 Canadian range.

The Junior Suites, which have vaulted ceilings, fireplaces, spa or soaking tubs, balconies, and queen-sized beds, carry rates in the high $300 Canadian range. Jacuzzi Rooms, all of which have spa tubs for two in the living area, are offered in the low $300 Canadian range. The Standard Rooms are in the high $200 Canadian range. Rates at the Aerie are considerably less from January through most of April.

DAYTIME DIVERSIONS

On SALT SPRING ISLAND, the bustling village of Ganges
is a short walk away from Hastings House. The town's
business center, perfect for afternoon strolling, is home to
several local arts-and-crafts galleries and cafes. A weekly
farmers' market operates in Centennial Park on Saturday.
A public tennis court, a swimming pool, and a golf course
are accessible from both inns in Ganges.

For quiet picnics on Salt Spring Island, our innkeepers
recommend Mount Maxwell's Lookout Point, northwest of
Ganges, and Ruckle Park on the island's southeastern coast.
Near Ruckle Park (McLennon Drive off Beaver Point Road)
is a dry-flower farm called Everlasting Summer. Nose Point,
at the tip of Long Harbour, a short drive from Ganges, is a
remote peninsula accessible only on foot; it affords spectacular vistas of the gulf waterways and passing ferries.

GALIANO ISLAND is a narrow slip of land with a pop-
ulation of fewer than a thousand. Most commercial activity
is confined to the southern end of the island, near the
Sturdies Bay ferry terminal. There's a nine-hole golf course
on Ellis Road off Sturdies Bay Road, and a short drive
away on the southern coast is lush Montague Provincial
Park. Visit with the locals over morning coffee, or lunch at
Spanish Hills General Store on the island's northwest end.

TABLES FOR TWO

On SALT SPRING ISLAND, we recommend the romantic
dining room at Hastings House (jackets required for men).
The menu here changes frequently but always features
fresh produce from the inn's large garden. If you'd prefer
to venture into Ganges for dinner, try House Piccolo on
Hereford Avenue. Quarrystone House innkeepers Kelly and
Barry Kazakoff also operate the Oyster Catcher Seafood
Bar and Grille in Ganges.

Our top choices for a romantic dinner on GALIANO
ISLAND are the dining rooms of our featured inns. Woodstone
Country Inn, which serves varied entrees ranging from trout
to pork, boasts a bucolic meadow view from the dining room.
The restaurant at Galiano Inn offers a view of the gulf.

FERRY INFORMATION

BC Ferries provides service to gulf islands from Swartz
Bay north of Victoria, from Vancouver, and from Tsawwassen,
south of Vancouver. For a ferry schedule, call (250) 386-
3431, or log on to www.bcferries.bc.ca.

THE CANADIAN GULF ISLANDS

THE FACTS

Four rooms, each with private bath, gas fireplace, and patio or balcony; two with spa tubs for two. Complimentary breakfast served at large communal table or delivered to your room. Disabled access. Two-night minimum stay required during weekends and holiday periods. Moderate to expensive.

GETTING THERE

From Vesuvius Bay Road (from ferry), drive to Sunset Drive and turn left. Follow to inn on left.

QUARRYSTONE HOUSE BED AND BREAKFAST
1340 Sunset Drive
Salt Spring Island, BC V8K 1E2
Canada
Telephone: (250) 537-5980;
toll-free: (866) 537-5980
Web site: www.quarrystone.com

QUARRYSTONE HOUSE BED AND BREAKFAST

With well over one hundred inns vying for attention on this small island, it took some work to search out the best. It's a duty we accepted with pleasure, to say the least. One of our new favorites is Quarrystone House, which makes up for its small size with large helpings of hospitality and romantic potential.

Situated on the north end of the island about a half dozen miles from the Vesuvius ferry, the inn hugs a ridge on five rolling acres overlooking Stonecutters Bay, Stuart Channel, and the beautiful countryside. At the time of our travels, sheep grazed on the property, along with a resident pony.

ROOMS FOR ROMANCE

Unlike many small inns where guests share space with the innkeeper, Quarrystone's four suites are located in a separate building that's connected by a patio to the main house. There are two on the main level and two upstairs. Each has either an ocean-view patio or balcony.

The smallest downstairs room is Flagstone (mid $100 Canadian range), which has a queen-sized bed, a one-person spa tub, a gas stove, a small wicker sofa, and a private patio. Next door is Gallery (mid $100 Canadian range), a two-room suite. The bedroom holds a king-sized bed and a second small room has a twin bed. This room also has a patio, a gas stove, and a single spa tub.

For a special romantic getaway, we recommend Treetops or Stonecutters, the two second-floor rooms (high $100 Canadian range), which offer spa tubs for two placed at the rear of the bedrooms. The Treetops room has a queen-sized bed and a gas fireplace, and the spa is set under a window with a view. Stonecutters has a gas potbellied stove next to a king-sized bed. Each of these rooms has a large covered balcony with a table and chairs and a spectacular water view.

Rooms at Quarrystone feature televisions and videocassette players hidden in pine amoires and are equipped with refrigerators and microwaves.

THE FACTS

Seventeen rooms and suites and one cottage, each with private bath, fireplace, minibar, and compact disc player; televisions available on request. Complimentary English breakfast served in dining room. Complimentary tea and refreshments served in afternoon; formal and casual dining room offering multicourse dinners (jackets required for men in formal dining room) for an extra charge. Disabled access. Two-night minimum stay during weekends and holiday periods. Deluxe.

GETTING THERE

Ferries call on Salt Spring Island at three different ports. Consequently, there are three different sets of directions. Vesuvius and Long Harbour are closest ferry terminals to inn. Inn is just west of Ganges village on Upper Ganges Road. Innkeepers will send detailed ferry and driving directions along with your reservation confirmation.

Hastings House
160 Upper Ganges Road
Salt Spring Island, BC V8K 2S2
Canada
Telephone: (250) 537-2362;
toll-free: (800) 661-9255
Web site: www.hastingshouse.com

HASTINGS HOUSE

In every region, one special destination sets the romantic standard. In the Canadian gulf islands, Hastings House tops our list. From every vantage point—inside and out—this quintessential country inn is flawless.

ROOMS FOR ROMANCE

Formerly a private estate, Hastings House has grown in recent years as more and more travelers discover Salt Spring Island and the refined elegance of this country house hotel. The property consists of seventeen rooms and suites, and a three-bedroom cottage, spread among a handful of charming buildings.

Among these is Post Cottage (mid to upper $500 Canadian range), a lovingly refurbished, pear-tree-shaded garden cottage (with woodstove), which originally functioned as the island's Hudson Bay trading post many years ago.

We sampled one of the two Farmhouse suites (mid $500 Canadian range) contained within a beautifully restored two-story structure offering views of Ganges and its placid harbor. In each, the bottom level is a living room with a couch, chairs, a fireplace, a wet bar, and a full bathroom. At the top of the stairs is a large bedroom with a spectacular water view and another full bathroom.

Two other favorite rooms are Sealoft and Hayloft (mid $400 Canadian range), located in a rustic building called the Barn. Sealoft is an upper-level room with an open brick fireplace and a romantic skylit bathroom; it also offers a peek at the harbor. Hayloft, also on the upper level, looks out over a meadow to the forest and is equipped with skylights and a woodburning stove.

Each of the five dazzling Deluxe Suites (mid $500 Canadian range) offers a gas fireplace, a heated tile floor, and a bathroom with an elegant soaking tub and a separate shower for two.

If the peak-season rates (mid-June through mid-October) noted above don't fit your budget, consider scheduling a visit at another time of the year, when tariffs at Hastings House drop substantially.

THE FACTS

Three rooms, each with private bath, wood stove, and balcony. Complimentary full breakfast served at communal table; continental breakfast can be delivered to your room. Complimentary tea and refreshments served every afternoon. No disabled access. Two-night minimum stay July through September and during all holiday weekends. Moderate to expensive.

GETTING THERE

Inn is located about ten minutes by automobile from Ganges. From Ganges, drive south and turn left onto Beddis Road. Follow Beddis Road for approximately 4 miles and turn left on Miles Avenue. Follow Miles Avenue to inn.

BEDDIS HOUSE

Beddis House is a romantic island getaway just waiting to be discovered—but only by three couples at a time. The inn's trio of rooms are hidden away in a newer carriage house built about a century after the construction of the property's centerpiece: a handsome farmhouse built in 1900. The heritage home, built by one of the island's first settlers, is set on lush grounds between a private beach on Georgia Strait and an age-old apple orchard.

Breakfast is served in the farmhouse dining room, and afternoon tea and refreshments are taken in the parlor or, weather permitting, outdoors.

ROOMS FOR ROMANCE

The Gingham and Butterflies rooms (mid to upper $100 Canadian range) occupy the downstairs portion of the carriage house. A queen-sized four-poster bed dominates the Butterflies room, which is also furnished with two rocking chairs and a wood stove. The French doors open onto your own deck.

Next door is Gingham with two extra-long iron twin beds, which happily can be joined to create a spacious king on request. Berber carpeting warms the hardwood floor, and a wood stove warms the room.

For special romantic getaways, we recommend the spacious Rose Bower room (around $200 Canadian), a luxury penthouse with a king-sized pencil-post cherry-wood bed, a matching armoire, and a sitting area with a long, cushy couch. Taking advantage of the island's temperate climate, this room boasts a large private balcony overlooking the water. The front window provides a lovely view of the inn's garden.

BEDDIS HOUSE

131 Miles Avenue
Salt Spring Island, BC V8K 2E1
Canada
Telephone: (250) 537-1028;
toll-free: (866) 537-1028
Web site: www.saltspring.com/beddishouse

THE FACTS

Eleven rooms, each with private bath, fireplace, and tele-phone. Complimentary breakfast served in restaurant. Restaurant, bar, and spa. Room service. Disabled access. Two-night minimum stay on weekends and holidays. Expensive.

GETTING THERE

Galiano Island is a fifty-minute ferry ride from Tsawwassen. Inn is located a short walk from the Sturdies Bay ferry landing. Inn staff will pick up guests at landing. No car is necessary

GALIANO INN

Situated on Sturdies Bay immediately adjacent to the ferry landing, the Galiano Inn provides a welcoming and impressive site to visitors—especially those who've had the foresight to book one of the luxurious rooms here.

The initial visual centerpiece for this coastal compound is a romantic restaurant and lounge with expansive windows and atrium-style seating overlooking the boats and whales in Active Pass, with Mount Baker and distant islands providing a dramatic backdrop. There's also a guest lounge, an art gallery, and a library. A day spa offering massages and other personal services is the most recent addition.

ROOMS FOR ROMANCE

If the restaurant and other public areas captured your attention, wait until you see your room. All eleven were created as if with our romantic criteria in mind. Decorated in Mediterranean style, they're spacious and luxurious, featuring fireplaces and balconies or terraces with inspirational water views.

The "corner king" suites (mid $200 Canadian range) are our favorites. These units have king-sized beds and spa tubs for two as well as showers.

Offered in the low $200 Canadian range, the "deluxe queen" rooms feature queen-sized wrought-iron canopied beds, and sitting areas with wing chairs and fireplaces. Rooms have large soaking tubs along with separate showers. The inn's "superior queen" rooms carry rates in the $200 Canadian range.

The inn also offers nature and island tours as well as whale watching excursions.

Galiano Inn
134 Madrona Drive (P.O. Box S24-C47)
Sturdies Bay, Galiano Island, BC VON 1PO
Canada
Telephone: (250) 539-3388;
toll-free: (877) 530-3939
Web site: www.galianoinn.com

THE FACTS

Thirteen rooms, each with private bath; most with fireplaces; several with tubs for two. Complimentary full breakfast served in dining room; complimentary tea and refreshments served in sitting room every afternoon; restaurant. Disabled access. Two-night minimum stay required from July through October and during holiday weekends. Moderate to expensive.

GETTING THERE

From Sturdies Bay ferry landing, follow Sturdies Bay Road for 2 miles (follow signs to Montague Harbor) to inn drive on left.

Woodstone Country Inn
Georgeson Bay Road (R.R. 1)
Galiano Island, BC VON 1PO
Canada
Telephone: (250) 539-2022
Web site: www.gulfislands.com/woodstone

WOODSTONE COUNTRY INN

This luxury hideaway, located at the heart of charming Galiano Island, celebrated its tenth anniversary at the turn of this new century. Its birthday brought new furnishings and gardens even more profuse than when we first happened by in the early years. The Woodstone Country Inn is reason enough to hop a ferry with that special someone and head for Galiano. And with gorgeous rooms starting at just over $100 Canadian, it's one of the best bargains in the gulf islands. You won't even mind passing up gulf views for the inn's green vistas of forest and meadowland.

Although the drive down the wooded road to the inn might have you anticipating rustic and funky, don't be fooled. This bright, luxurious, contemporary showplace strikes quite a contrast to some of the humble structures you'll pass on the drive up. The inn is a long two-story structure with soaring windows, perched at the edge of an expansive meadow used at certain times of the year for horse dressage training.

A country inn in the best sense, Woodstone is one of those special destinations where you'll be tempted to park the car for the length of your visit. Not only will you be treated to a full country breakfast, but wonderful multicourse gourmet dinners are served each evening in the inn's dining room (for an extra charge). This popular dining spot (it's open to nonguests as well) also features live piano or guitar music.

ROOMS FOR ROMANCE

The guest rooms are situated on two levels along main hallways. Those at the rear of the inn face the meadow and distant forest, while the rooms facing front have views of trees beyond the parking area. The first-floor rooms have small (but not completely private) patios.

The rooms facing the meadow emerged as our favorites, not only because of the inspirational views but because of the amenities. They are equipped with fireplaces and with soaking tubs big enough for two.

Among the most expensive (mid $100 Canadian range) are Wild Rose and Hawthorn, both remote corner rooms. In Wild Rose, on the second floor, a large dormer window frames the pastoral panorama, also visible from the king-sized bed. Hawthorn is furnished with a wicker love seat and chair and has twin beds that can be joined to create a king. Both rooms have large soaking tubs and love seats.

Dogwood (around $200 Canadian) is a newer room whose twenty feet of windows boast a meadow view, and it holds a spa tub for two and a shower, a fireplace, and a queen-sized bed.

The other two first-floor rooms with a view of the valley are Lilac and Lily (both in the low to mid $100 Canadian range). Both have large soaking tubs. On the second floor facing the valley are Iris and Sunflower, both with queen-sized beds. The rates for these rooms are in the low to mid $100 Canadian range.

The forest-view rooms (in the low $100 Canadian range) with fireplaces are Foxglove, Trillium, and Poppy. Foxglove has a double bed; all other rooms along this side of the inn have queen-sized beds.

DAYTIME DIVERSIONS

In VANCOUVER, Stanley Park is the primary attraction.
One of the world's most beautiful urban parks, this lush
peninsula encompasses one thousand acres. The five-mile
pedestrian and bike path along the seawall is a great way
to see the park.

The arts and history of the region are showcased in
the University of British Columbia Museum of Anthropology
on the UBC campus, the Vancouver Museum on Chestnut
Street, and the Vancouver Art Gallery in the City Centre.

The Bloedel Floral Conservatory atop Queen Elizabeth
Park features a huge, all-season dome-covered garden
containing five hundred varieties of plants.

Other romantic pastimes include a summertime ride
on a chairlift at Grouse Mountain, a stroll through Dr. Sun
Yat-sen Classical Chinese Garden in Vancouver's Chinatown,
and a visit to Capilano Suspension Bridge and Park.

If you're staying at Laburnum Cottage Bed and
Breakfast, there are tennis courts and a nine-hole golf
course three blocks away. Grouse Mountain ski resort is a
five-minute drive from the inn.

Whistler resort, voted the world's most popular ski
area, is about seventy-five miles north of Vancouver.
Blackcomb and Whistler Mountains boast more skiable
terrain than any other North American ski area. In the
warmer months, visitors choose from bicycling (there are
more than a dozen rental shops), fishing (in five lakes and
numerous streams), golf (the Arnold Palmer–designed
course is rated among the world's best), hiking, boating,
and horseback riding. Whistler Village is a collection of
Alpine-style shops, restaurants, and condominium complexes set along cobbled pathways.

TABLES FOR TWO

In VANCOUVER, Cin Cin (Robson Street), Le Crocodile
(Burrard Street), and Rain City Grill (Denman Street) are
highly recommended by our innkeepers. Also recommended
are Raintree (Alberni Street and Cardero) for Pacific
Northwest dishes, and Mescalero (Bidwell and Davie
Streets) for Southwestern cuisine. The restaurants atop
Grouse Mountain offer incredible views.

Our WHISTLER innkeepers recommend Rimrock Cafe
on Whistler Road and La Rua on Blackcomb Way.

SOUTHWEST BRITISH COLUMBIA

THE FACTS

Two suites, each with private bath and deck. Complimentary full breakfast delivered to your room. Hot tub. No disabled access. No minimum night stay requirement. Moderate.

GETTING THERE

From Vancouver, follow Trans-Canada Highway (Highway 1) to Abbotsford Mission exit. Drive north on Abbotsford Mission Highway (Highway 11) to Lougheed Highway (Highway 7) and turn right. Follow east to Morris Valley Road and turn left. Follow to four-way stop and turn left again. Follow road for 1 mile and turn left at inn's gated entrance.

CHRISTOPHER'S, A WOODLAND BED AND BREAKFAST
14400 Echo Lake Road (P.O. Box 97)
Harrison Mills, BC V0M 1L0
Canada
Telephone: (888) 732-6627
Web site: www.christopherswoodlands.com

CHRISTOPHER'S, A WOODLAND BED AND BREAKFAST

With only two rooms, Christopher's may be the smallest of our Northwest discoveries. However, in terms of romantic potential, it delivers in a big way. Set on a rock face, surrounded by trees, and overlooking a tranquil mountain lake, the inn strikes an awe-inspiring pose.

And while the forty-acre setting affords multiple opportunities to enjoy the outdoors, it's also a perfect destination for simply unwinding and enjoying each other's company. In fact, proprietor Leona Holland, formerly the innkeeper at nearby Rowena's (see next listing), reports that many traveling twosomes arriving with hiking boots, golf clubs, and bikes never make it much beyond their private guest room decks or the inn's hot tub in a private forested setting. "When I see that, I know it's working," she says proudly.

ROOMS FOR ROMANCE

Both rooms have private view decks and private entrances. Our favorite of the pair has to be the upstairs Stellar Suite (mid $100 Canadian range). This romantic roost boasts a king-sized cherry-wood sleigh bed, at the foot of which is a sitting area with two Craftsman-style chairs facing a free-standing stove. There are also a small table and chairs, where you'll enjoy the breakfast that's delivered to your room. And tucked into a corner under the sloping ceiling is a tile-sided and -backed soaking tub for two. The bathroom is equipped with a shower, and the deck offers a fabulous lake view. There are also a coffeemaker and refrigerator in this suite.

On the main floor is the Victorian-styled Master Suite (low to mid $100 Canadian range), which has a large deck with a garden view and a partial lake view. A bit smaller than the Stellar Suite, this room has a king-sized bed and a windowed corner seating area with two comfortable wing chairs facing a freestanding stove. There's a clawfoot tub (designed for one) in the room, while the bathroom has a shower for two. This room also has a table and chairs.

THE FACTS

Nine rooms, seven with private baths; two rooms with shared bath. Complimentary full breakfast served in solarium at tables for two or more. Swimming pool, hot tub, and eighteen-hole golf course. Restaurant serves dinner daily; lunch and brunch served on certain days. Disabled access. No minimum night stay requirement. Expensive to deluxe.

GETTING THERE

From Vancouver, follow Trans-Canada Highway (Highway 1) to Abbotsford Mission exit. Drive north on Abbotsford Mission Highway (Highway 11) to Lougheed Highway (Highway 7) and turn right. Follow to Morris Valley Road and turn left. Inn is on right. Allow for a one-and-a-half to two-hour drive from Vancouver.

ROWENA'S INN ON THE RIVER
14282 Morris Valley Road
Harrison Mills, BC V0M 1L0
Canada
Telephone: (604) 796-0234;
toll-free: (800) 661-5108
Web site: www.rowenasinn.com

ROWENA'S INN ON THE RIVER

Your own private river mountain cottage awaits at this remote destination, and the best part is that it's just a couple of hours away from bustling Vancouver.

Rowena's, owned by the Pretty family since 1920, is a handsome estate that has operated as an inn since 1995. In addition to a romantic on-site dining room that's open daily for lunch and dinner to locals as well as guests, this 160-acre property boasts an eighteen-hole golf course. A seventy-foot-long swimming pool and a river-view communal hot tub are among other guest amenities. The Hemlock Valley ski area is about ten miles away.

Rowena's Inn on the River is a destination-type getaway. Don't expect to find lots of shopping and dining alternatives, as the nearby hamlet of Harrison Mills consists of little more than a gas station and pub. However, judging by the romantic ambience of your cabin by the water, we don't think you'll be starved for entertainment.

ROOMS FOR ROMANCE

The five upstairs rooms in the main house have king- or queen-sized beds. Decorated in Victorian style, these accommodations are each equipped with a corner table and two chairs. Pete's Room, Bettyanne's Room, and Ivan's Room (mid $200 Canadian range) overlook the river. Rowena's Room and Charlie's Room (low $200 Canadian range) have wooded views. Note that Ivan's Room shares a bath with Rowena's Room. Guests staying in the main house take their breakfast around a communal table in a pretty solarium.

For a special romantic getaway celebration, we recommend the four cottages (low $200 to low $300 Canadian range) that overlook a little trout pond and the adjacent Harrison River. These spacious wood-paneled charmers have bay windows, queen-sized pencil-post beds, tables and chairs, and easy chairs placed before handsome stone wood-burning fireplaces. In the large bathroom you'll find a spa tub for two and a separate shower. A full breakfast is delivered each morning. You may also request that dinner, available at extra cost, be served in your cottage.

WEST END GUEST HOUSE

1362 Haro Street
Vancouver, BC V6E 1G2
Canada
Telephone: (604) 681-2889
Web site: www.westendguesthouse.com

THE FACTS

Eight rooms, each with private bath, bathrobes, slippers, television, and telephone. Complimentary full breakfast served in dining room or delivered to guests in rooms 1 and 2; complimentary tea and sherry served each afternoon. Bicycles available free to guests. Multinight minimum stay required at certain times of year. No disabled access. Smoking is not permitted. Moderate to expensive.

GETTING THERE

From Highway 99 northbound, follow highway (Oak Street) into Vancouver. Turn left on Broadway/Ninth Avenue. Turn right on Granville Street and proceed over Granville Street Bridge. Take Seymour Street exit to Robson Street and turn left. Turn left on Broughton Street and drive one block to inn. From Tsawwassen ferry terminal, follow Highway 17 to Highway 99, then follow above directions.

WEST END GUEST HOUSE

Relaxing in the enchanting and intimate West End Guest House, it's hard to imagine that this bustling district of Vancouver is one of the most densely populated areas in the world. West End Guest House, with its engaging Victorian and Edwardian facade painted a fanciful raspberry, is certainly an attention getter among the West End's many condominium and apartment complexes.

Originally the grand residence of Vancouver's first professional photographer, the turn-of-the-century home has been expertly refurbished with just the right balance of vintage charm and modern comforts to make it ideally suited for cozy romantic encounters. Its also within easy striking distance of all that Vancouver has to offer. We explored Stanley Park using the inn's bikes, and strolled six blocks to the heart of downtown.

ROOMS FOR ROMANCE

We'll start our romantic tour on the third floor, where two rooms sit under sloping eaves. This isn't a dingy attic. Room 2, known as the Grand Queen Suite (mid $200 Canadian range), offers a peek of the city and distant mountains through the windows and skylight. A sitting area at the foot of an angled queen-sized brass bed is furnished with a sofa and a 1930s-era stuffed armchair. There's also a gas fireplace, and a small dining table where guests may enjoy breakfast. The bathroom has a clawfoot slipper-style soaking tub and a shower; the inn's other rooms have stall showers.

Room 1, known as the King Room (low $200 Canadian range), faces the rear and is bright and comfortable, decorated with a pretty, deep-green carpet, coordinating wallpaper, two armchairs, and a king-sized bed.

Raccoons and squirrels have been known to scale the fig tree that grows outside the bay window of room 4 (mid $100 Canadian range), on the second floor. This room is furnished with dark antiques and old photos. A small table and two chairs sit near the window.

Room 5 (high $100 Canadian range), also on the second floor, is a front-facing room with a bay window. In addition to an ornate carved mahogany bed, the room is equipped with a lovely reproduction mahogany settee upholstered in red velvet. Room 8, on the lower level, has a steam shower.

Rooms 6 and 7 have double beds. All others have queen-sized beds; all beds are brass, with feather mattresses.

THE FACTS

Six rooms, each with private bath; five with gas fireplaces.
Complimentary full breakfast served at communal table.
Disabled access. No minimum night stay requirement.
Moderate to expensive.

GETTING THERE

From Highway 99 northbound, cross Lion's Gate Bridge,
turn right on Marine Drive North, left on Capilano Road,
right on Paisley Road, right on Phillip Avenue, right on
Woods Drive, and left on Terrace Avenue to inn on left.

LABURNUM COTTAGE BED AND BREAKFAST
1388 Terrace Avenue
North Vancouver, BC V7R 1B4
Canada
Telephone: (604) 988-4877;
toll-free: (888) 207-8901
Web site: www.vancouver-bc.com/
laburnumcottagebb

LABURNUM COTTAGE BED AND BREAKFAST

After moving to Vancouver from Europe, the original owners of this suburban estate worked to fashion an environment reminiscent of their homeland. This included the creation of the elaborate gardens and summer cottage that today form the centerpiece of Laburnum Cottage Bed and Breakfast.

Hidden at the end of a street in a quiet North Vancouver neighborhood and bordered by a protected forest, the inn might easily be mistaken by passersby for another family home, which is precisely what it was when Delphine Masterton and her late husband raised five children here. The Mastertons first opened their home to guests in anticipation of the Vancouver World Exposition in 1986, and the rest is innkeeping history.

We try very hard not to play favorites when traveling the romantic road, but it's difficult after making the acquaintance of an innkeeper like Delphine Masterton. She is the guiding light of Laburnum Cottage and the warmest hostess we met during our travels through the Northwest.

ROOMS FOR ROMANCE

Three of the inn's accommodations are on the second floor of the main house. All have queen-sized beds and private baths with small shower stalls. Our room for a night, the Queen Anne (upper $100 Canadian range), overlooked the rear garden as well as a little-used front garden.

Also on this level are the Rose Room (upper $100 Canadian range), with Sanderson wall coverings, and Buttercup (mid $100 Canadian range), decorated in bright butter yellow. Many of the antique furnishings are heirlooms from Delphine's grandmother's home in England.

What was once the garage is now a large cottage called the Carriage House, (upper $100 Canadian range), furnished with a kitchen, a fireplace, wing chairs, a queen-sized bed, and a loft. The bathroom holds a large soaking tub.

We save our most hearty recommendation for the secluded Summerhouse Cottage (high $200 Canadian range), set against forestland at the edge of the back garden. Reached via a path that crosses a small creek over a red Oriental footbridge, Summerhouse was originally intended as a quiet place of family refuge. Alex Masterton later transformed the cottage into another bedroom for his growing family.

Summerhouse Cottage holds a small gas fireplace, a brass queen-sized bed, and a small sitting area. An old brass Turkish lantern hangs above the fireplace. There's also a kitchenette with a sink, a small refrigerator, a microwave, and an electric kettle. The cottage's bathroom is wall-papered and has a soaking tub.

Latticed windows face the inn's acclaimed garden, an ever-blooming sanctuary that overflows with flowers, trees, and shrubs.

THE FACTS

Eight rooms, each with private bath. Amenities include fresh flowers in your room. Complimentary full breakfast served at communal tables. Complimentary tea and refreshments served every afternoon; authentic Austrian dinners served on an occasional basis. (Inquire about dinner availability when you make your reservations.) Spa and sauna. Disabled access. Two-night minimum stay required on weekends. Golf, ski, and spa packages available. Moderate to expensive (summer rates are lower).

GETTING THERE

From northbound Highway 99, turn left on Nesters Road three-quarters of a mile past Whistler Village to inn. Whistler is approximately two hours from Vancouver and five hours from Seattle.

DURLACHER HOF
7055 Nesters Road
Whistler, BC V0N 1B7
Canada
Telephone: (604) 932-1924
Web site: www.durlacherhof.com

DURLACHER HOF

While Whistler's pervasive Alpine architectural motif ends abruptly at the front door of many local hostelries, Durlacher Hof serves up a complete authentic Austrian experience, from the ornate exterior trimmings to the *kaiserschmarren* (sweet raisin pancake) served at breakfast.

Situated a short walk from Whistler Village, Durlacher Hof boasts a classic Tyrolean facade that combines gleaming white plaster walls with an elaborately carved balcony and wooden beams. The inn takes its name from owners Erika and Peter Durlacher, both of Austrian descent. Guests who elect to dine at the inn are treated to hearty homestyle dishes from the Durlachers' Austrian homeland.

ROOMS FOR ROMANCE

Popular among Canadian and American visitors, the inn is decorated with charming-but-sturdy pine furnishings—no delicate antiques here. The beds are covered with goose-down duvets and luxury linens.

The Executive Junior Suite (mid $200 Canadian range) occupies a spacious corner of the second floor. The sitting room has two comfortable easy chairs, a wet bar, and a small desk, and the bedroom is equipped with a king-sized four-poster bed. There's a spa tub for one in the bathroom. A half French door opens to a balcony area with a table and chairs. The Whistler, Wedge, and Blackcomb Mountains are part of the impressive view.

The Durlachers also offer two cozy rooms under the eaves on the third floor (each in the mid $200 Canadian range). These are perfect for couples on their honeymoon or celebrating an anniversary. Both have queen-sized four-poster pine beds with duvets, and French doors opening to Juliet balconies. The bathroom in each of these third-floor rooms has a large soaking tub for two.

On arrival, guests are invited to trade their street shoes for a cozy pair of hut slippers, which are made from boiled wool.

Traffic on busy Nesters Road can sometimes be heard from the second-floor rooms during the summer months when the windows are open. Noise isn't a problem in the winter.

THE FACTS

Five rooms, each with private bath. Complimentary full breakfast served at tables for two. Fixed-price dinners offered on an occasional basis. (Inquire when you make your reservation about dinner availability.) Spa. No disabled access. Two-night minimum stay required during weekends; three-night minimum required during holiday periods. Moderate.

GETTING THERE

From northbound Highway 99, turn at Bayshores, first subdivision on right. Turn right at "T" (Cheakamus) and follow to end, bearing right onto Clifftop Lane. Continue up hill to inn's sign on right.

One of Whistler's newest bed-and-breakfast destinations, Inn at Clifftop Lane is also one of the area's better bargains, offering romantic rooms in the mid to high $100 Canadian range during ski season. When the snow goes away, room rates melt as well.

Constructed in the late 1990s in the chalet style so popular in Whistler, Inn at Clifftop Lane is among the most highly rated inns in this popular village. That's no small feat in a community boasting a staggering five thousand-plus guest rooms.

The inn is situated on a quiet street, only one kilometer from the gondola at Whistler Creekside, which has undergone considerable renovation in recent times. The enchanting and pedestrian-friendly Whistler Village is about four kilometers from the inn.

ROOMS FOR ROMANCE

Comfortable and furnished with contemporary and antique pieces, the inn's five guest rooms are a great place to relax, unwind, and get cozy after a day on the slopes of the mountain. The beds are dressed in luxury and complemented by embroidered linens and handcrafted quilts and throws.

Rooms One and Five have mountain views; the others look into the trees. Room Three is the inn's largest, and features a king-sized bed and a balcony. Room Four has a double bed.

Whether you're ski-weary, romantic, or both, you'll appreciate the spa tubs in each room. Although the tubs are designed for one, they're deep, and the two of you might just fit in a pinch. Each room is also equipped with a television and a videocassette player. The inn has a tape library.

There's also a covered communal spa set on the patio at the rear of the property. Stairs from here lead to the surrounding forest and a deck with a log gazebo.

INN AT CLIFFTOP LANE
2828 Clifftop Lane
Whistler, BC V0N 1B2
Canada
Telephone: (604) 938-1229;
toll-free: (888) 281-2929
Web site: www.innatclifftop.com

Index